Michel Foucault

Michel Foucault

By David R. Shumway

University Press of Virginia
Charlottesville and London

THE UNIVERSITY PRESS OF VIRGINIA
Copyright 1989 by G. K. Hall & Co.

First paperback edition 1992

Library of Congress Cataloging-in-Publication Data

Shumway, David R.
  Michel Foucault. — 1st pbk. ed.
    p.   cm.
  Includes bibliographical references (p.   ) and index.
  ISBN 0-8139-1415-9 (paper)
  1. Foucault, Michel.   I. Title.
B2430.F724S55   1992
194—dc20   92–13504
                                        CIP

Printed in the United States of America

For Linda Colantonio Shumway

Contents

About the Author

David Shumway is assistant professor of literary and cultural studies in the English Department of Carnegie Mellon University. He received his B.A. from New College of Hofstra University and his M.A. and Ph.D. from Indiana University. His specialties are literary and cultural theory and American studies. He has published numerous articles in scholarly journals and collections. He is the current director and a founding member of GRIP, the Group for Research into the Institutionalization and Professionalization of literary studies. He is at work on a genealogy of American literature as an academic field.

Preface

Along with Jacques Derrida, Jacques Lacan, and Roland Barthes, Michel Foucault was one of the most significant voices in poststructuralism. Although poststructuralism is understood in the United States mainly as literary theory, of those mentioned above only Barthes was a literary critic. Poststructuralism is really a category of convenience that names at most an intellectual tendency and perhaps merely a historical moment in French thought. It is thus impossible to articulate a set of doctrines that all poststructuralists share. Of the major figures, however, Foucault fits least comfortably in the category. What distinguishes him from the other three is the importance of history in his work. While their theories tend to make historical knowledge impossible, Foucault finds new ways to write history. It is, I think, this historical dimension that has enabled Foucault's work to have a much broader impact than that of the other poststructuralists. In addition to literary theory, Foucault has influenced the disciplines of philosophy and history as well as all of the social science disciplines.

But if this wide influence makes Foucault a figure of major importance, it also suggests the difficulties one might have in coming to his work for the first time. Although Foucault was trained as a philosopher and at times held teaching positions in philosophy, his work is not philosophy in any of its usual forms. Although the word *"l'histoire"* appears in the titles of many of his works, his histories abandon many of the conventional assumptions of historians, such as the usual continuities of historical time. While most of his books are almost baroque in their use of concrete detail, the materials that he writes about are likely to be unfamiliar even to other specialists. Finally, Foucault has had great impact because his work repeatedly challenges our assumptions, beliefs, and expectations. As most poststructuralist theory suggests, genuinely new thought must be new discourse. Thus Foucault writes in a style and in a vocabulary that is strange to most readers.

Having taught Foucault's works to both graduate and undergraduate students over the past four years, I came to this book—which is meant to be accessible to readers who are not experts—

with an acute sense of these difficulties. My major strategy in trying to overcome these difficulties has been to call attention to those things in Foucault's work that do tend to be stumbling blocks. I have also sought to find examples from a range of disciplines and materials to use as illustrations. I have tried to avoid, on the other hand, oversimplifying Foucault's ideas, but invariably a book of this kind must exclude much of the richness and complexity of the original works. This book is not meant as a substitute for them, however, but as a means of entry into their discursive world.

I begin my survey of that world with a discussion of authorship. Foucault's treatment of that concept is often lumped in with the more general poststructuralist attack on the author best represented by Barthes. After distinguishing Foucault's use of the term, I discuss his career as an author. Chapter 2 takes up the discursive strategies that characterize Foucault's writing: reversal, discontinuity, specificity, and exteriority. These strategies are partly responsible for the strangeness of Foucault's writing and, by mentioning them up front, I hope to give the reader rudimentary directions for getting around in the territory to be covered. Chapter 3 focuses on the historical nominalism of Foucault's treatment of madness in *Madness and Civilization* and concludes with a discussion of the structuralism of *The Birth of the Clinic* and the notion of gaze. Chapter 4, the longest chapter, tries to provide a map of the historical and philosophical maze that is *The Order of Things*. I argue that this most famous of Foucault's works is a significant rewriting of modern intellectual history in the West. Chapter 5 looks at Foucault's methods, archaeology and geneology, as ways of reconceiving knowledge and its divisions, and the writing of history. *Discipline and Punish*, a book that provides a radical reconception of the operations of power in modern society, is the subject of chapter 6. Power is also a significant issue in chapter 7, which focuses mainly on volume 1 of *The History of Sexuality* and its rewriting of the modern period as an era of the proliferation, rather than repression, of sexuality.

My conclusion points to some possible consequences of Foucault's work not only for several branches of knowledge, but also for the lives and commitments of individuals. What for me distinguishes Foucault's work most fundamentally from that of Derrida, Lacan, Barthes, and that of most American poststructuralists is its potential to help remake the social and political structures of the twentieth century. By making us aware that a concatenation of power, knowledge, practices, institutions, and even the very bodies of individuals forms the structure of domination today, Foucault leads us to reconceive politics and to try to invent new strategies of struggle, but never to abandon oppositional practice.

This book owes much to others from whom I have learned. I first read Foucault in the context of the early work of the GRIP project including regular discussions with Jim Sosnoski, Steve Nimis, Jim Fanto, and Patricia Harkin. Later, discussions with other members of GRIP—especially Paul Bové, Jonathan Arac, and Karlis Racevskis—helped me to refine my thinking about Foucault, and my work in the project allowed me to see the power of his thought for redescribing the relations between the formations of knowledge and social institutions. Conversations with Linda Singer, Fran Bartkowski, and Brian McHale were also helpful and influential. I may have learned the most important things about how to write this book, however, from my students Andrea Blaustein, Margaret Halter, Sally Magargee, Karen O'Kane, Alice Rabinowitz, Gary Schaffer, Jean Sieper, John Tsgaris, and Tracy Valline, most members of a graduate seminar on Foucault I offered in the fall of 1986. They were the initial audience for the approaches to Foucault I have used here. Their difficulties in understanding Foucault helped me to better formulate the strategies I have used, and their insights taught me to understand him better.

Special thanks are extended to Dana Polan and Karlis Racevskis who each read earlier drafts of the manuscript and provided useful commentary, and to my editor, David O'Connell, who in 1984 had faith in a young scholar with a part-time job and few publications.

David R. Shumway

Carnegie Mellon University

Chronology

1976 *History of Sexuality, Volume I: An Introduction.*

1980 *Herculine Barbin.*

1984 *The Use of Pleasure* and *The Care of the Self,* vols. 2 and 3 of *The History of Sexuality.*

1984 Dies, Paris, 24 June.

Chapter One

Foucault as an Author

There is considerable irony in the fact that Michel Foucault is now represented by a volume in the Twayne World Authors Series. For although it was Roland Barthes who proclaimed the death of the author, it was Foucault who performed the autopsy. Or to be more exact in my use of metaphor, who examined the body that *seemed* to Barthes to be dead. In this introduction, I want to use Foucault's essay "What is an Author?" to illustrate the kind of thinking characteristic of Foucault, to explain why Foucault might be understood to object to this volume itself, and to present some information about Foucault's life.

The Problem of Authorship

When Roland Barthes discussed the death of the author, he was referring to what had already become a tradition in French literature since the poet Stéphane Mallarmé, who in the nineteenth century had insisted on re-placing the center of the reader's attention on language itself rather than on the individual who writes. Various movements within modernist literature also diminished the significance of the author by such means as the surrealists' advocacy of automatic writing, or Bertolt Brecht's "distancing" that placed the author as "a figurine at the far end of the literary stage."[1] During the middle part of this century in the United States, the New Criticism also de-emphasized the author by its assertion that the meaning of literary work could not be discovered in his extratextual life or intentions. Barthes argues that the reader lives where the author had lived before, but for "reader" we must read "critic," because Barthes wants to elevate the production of critical readings to a place of greater importance than the original texts.

Foucault, on the other hand, asks that we not repeat the empty slogan of "the death of the author," but instead that we "reexamine the empty space left by the author's disappearance."[2] To make sense

of "What is an Author?" we need to understand that the word
"author" is used there in at least two distinct ways. The author who
has disappeared, or who is dead, is that conception of the historical
individual as the guarantor of unity, intention, meaning, and other
transcendental qualities of a work. But Foucault also speaks of the
"author-function," which treats these qualities and the author who
supports them as "constructions" of discourse. A "construction"
might be thought of as an habitual way of thinking, the habit being
reinforced by the terms in which the thought occurs. Foucault
believes that most of our knowledge and experience of the world
takes place as the effect of these constructions. Foucault suggests
that the author-function, being such a habit, is not dead and is very
hard to kill. Even after we have stopped looking to the biography
or psychology of the actual historical writer as the source of a text's
meaning, we often continue to assume the unifying presence of an
author when we read fiction, poetry, and even philosophy. Foucault
accuses Jacques Derrida—and by implication, Barthes—of making
this mistake in the notion of *écriture,* that is, writing taken as the
primordial play of presence and absence, a system of signs independent of the intention or will of an author. *Écriture* is for Foucault
another way of preserving the sacred origin of writing or our belief
in its creative nature. In the notion of *écriture,* writing itself replaces
God or the author as an a priori that guarantees meaning beyond
discourse itself just as these two other a priori principles have. Thus
the search for hidden meaning continues to go on under the sign
of *écriture* just as it always has. Foucault has announced his opposition
to this "commentary,"[3] the sort of interpretation that searches for
deep or hidden meaning, and here he finds another way that philosophers and literary critics have kept it alive.

Rather than trying to relocate meaning in the reader or a metaphysics of writing, Foucault wants to examine the role of authorship as a convention of discourse. Foucault illustrates the
particular significance of authorship in a discussion of the ways in
which the name of the author differs in its function from other
proper names. An author's name does not simply designate or describe an individual, for it also designates and describes his works.
If we learn that someone named John Doe is not six feet tall, does
not have brown eyes, does not live in New York, and has never
contemplated suicide, the name "John Doe" continues to designate

the same person. But, as Foucault notes, the name "Shakespeare" is a good deal more problematic:

> The disclosure that Shakespeare was not born in the house that tourists now visit would not modify the functioning of the author's name, but, if it were proved that he had not written the sonnets that we attribute to him, this would . . . affect the manner in which the author's name functions. Moreover, if we establish that Shakespeare wrote Bacon's *Organon* and that the same author was responsible for both the works of Shakespeare and those of Bacon, we would have introduced a third type of alteration which completely modifies the functioning of the author's name." (*W* 122)

To say that John Doe never existed would merely be to assert that there was no one by the name of John Doe. To say that Shakespeare never existed suggests that several people have been mistakenly designated by this one name, or that the real author had none of the traits normally associated with Shakespeare.

The author's name is a form of classification that groups together certain texts and differentiates these texts from others. This classification not only distinguishes texts attributed to one author from those attributed to other authors, but also distinguishes them from all the texts that do not have authors. Foucault points out that although private letters, contracts, anonymous wall posters, etc., all have writers, they do not have authors. The author-function thus distinguishes certain discourses within society from other discourses. Among the texts grouped together under an author's name various relationships are established. Many of these relationships are disclosed in Saint Jerome's criteria for determining the attribution of texts. He specifies that the following kinds of texts ought to be removed from an author's oeuvre: 1) those inferior to the others; 2) those containing ideas in conflict with the others; 3) those whose style, diction, and syntax differ from that found in the others; 4) those containing references to events that happened after the author's death. These four rules posit the author as a standard of quality, a field of conceptual coherence, a stylistic unity, and a definite historical figure. While we would no longer blindly follow these rules in authenticating the works attributed to a particular author, Foucault argues that we continue to define authorship in a similar way. These relationships do not result merely from attributing discourse to an individual, but have to be actively constructed by readers, interpreters, and critics.

In addition to establishing certain relations between texts in an oeuvre, the author-function also carries three other features that distinguish authored from unauthored discourse. First, authorship makes discourse someone's property. Foucault associates this appropriation of discourse both with the need to punish those responsible for transgressive speech and with the more recent development of strict copyright laws. Speeches and books were once attributed to mythical figures or religious leaders, and were given real authors only when the discourse caused the author to be subject to punishment. Discourse was understood as action, not as property, and only "bad" actions warranted the public identification of the writer. Copyright laws ensured the attribution of discourse to an author, and thus gave writing a renewed sense of danger. Second, the author-function has differed historically and even among discourses within our own time. In an earlier period literary genres— stories, folk tales, epics, etc.—were repeated and revered without question of authorship. During the same period, however, scientific texts depended for their validity on the name of a wise man such as Hippocrates or Pliny. Sometime in the seventeenth and eighteenth centuries, this situation became reversed. Scientific writing became validated on the basis of a system of truths and methods of verification, but literary works were required to bear the name of an author or be classified as subliterary. Third, the author-function affects the way we read the pronouns in a text that refer to its writer or speaker. In texts without an author, we assume that the pronoun "I," for example, refers to a real speaker or writer. But in works of fiction told in the first person we assume that "I" refers to a sort of character, even if he is not a fully developed one such as Nick Carraway in *The Great Gatsby*. Foucault argues that such a disjunction between the "I" and the actual writer occurs in all authored discourses. Hence, in a mathematical treatise, the "I" of the preface is not the same as the "I" who solves a problem in the text itself. The first "I" is one whose particular circumstances led him to this project, who has intellectual debts to acknowledge, etc. The second "I" has no particular circumstances at all, for what he demonstrates will hold true for anyone who repeats his steps. Indeed, this "I" is often effaced, becoming "one" or "we."

Foucault's discussion of the author and the author-function illustrates the kinds of intellectual moves he characteristically makes. The most important of these is the shift in focus to discourse as the object of attention rather than as the medium of expression. As long as there is an author whose thoughts are said to be expressed in a text, our attention fixes on the author and not on the discourse. Foucault wants us to be concerned with the historical analysis of discourse and with its mode of existence: "the modifications and variations, within any culture, of modes of circulation, valorization, attribution, and appropriation" (*W* 137). Foucault's analysis of the author-function, the construction of the author within discourse, is an example of this shift of focus to the mode of existence of discourse. Hence in the future he would have us not repeat such questions as "Who is the real author?" or "What has he revealed of his most profound self in his language?" Rather, our concerns should be "Where does this discourse come from? How is it circulated? Who controls it?" or "What place does the discourse provide for speakers and listeners?" (*W* 138).

Given this orientation, Foucault might say that it is inevitable that this book you are now reading treats him as an author, in part because his writing has for better or worse been produced within a discourse that carries the author-function. It would come as no surprise to him that in the following pages I will show how Foucault's works are more or less unified. Although I will observe certain changes or contradictions among them, I will not dwell on these ruptures. Imagine if I did, what impression of Foucault most readers would come away with. He would be perceived as someone who could not make up his mind, and therefore as someone unworthy of our attention. He would be stigmatized as mad or foolish or simply inconsistent, all of which would render him trivial. Furthermore, Foucault's writing is difficult enough to understand without emphasizing its own contradictions. It is the purpose of studies written about authors to make sense of their work. To dwell on Foucault's contradictions would lead to the opposite end, even though one might be just as literally accurate in such an emphasis. The point is that the form of discourse I am engaged in here cannot be done without the assumption of the author's unity.

But I will do more here than render "Foucault" a name for a homogeneous group of texts. I will also treat him as a real, historical individual whose works to some extent express his personal circumstances. We might imagine Foucault resisting the personal more than he would resist the assumption of consistency in his works. Foucault managed to keep the details of his private life out of the public eye. Unlike Barthes or Jacques Derrida, Foucault left nothing in the way of autobiography. In the introduction to *The Archaeology of Knowledge,* Foucault said, "I am no doubt not the only one who writes in order to have no face. Do not ask who I am and do not ask me to remain the same: leave it to our bureaucrats and our police to see that our papers are in order."[4] To begin this volume, then, with a discussion of Foucault's career, is to treat him as an author in a sense that he seems to have tried to avoid all his life. Furthermore, he seems to have believed that we in the twentieth century were well on our way to writing this kind of author out of discourse. As my discussion of *The Order of Things* reveals, Foucault believes that we are now moving into an age that is quite different from that of the nineteenth and early twentieth centuries. Then writing and thought were understood as expressions of the self; now writing, thought, and the self have become the effects of discourse itself.

Nevertheless, I must assert that the conventions of authorship have not changed so much as Foucault would have perhaps liked to believe. The industry of biography does not seem to be grinding to a halt. On the contrary, each year seems to yield another raft of longer, more detailed biographies of authors. If it is no longer true that we read literary texts primarily to resurrect the psychic life of the author, biography remains a means by which people understand not just literary works, but those of thinkers like Foucault as well. Foucault's later work, in which discourse is no longer treated as strictly autonomous, suggests that he might well have understood the need for readers unfamiliar with his work to know that it was often a response to very real problems such as prison conditions or the treatment of homosexuals (Foucault was a homosexual). And since Foucault on several occasions acknowledged the influence of his teachers such as Jean Hyppolite and Georges Canguilhem, he might also see the need for readers to understand the intellectual-historical background of his work. Thus even if Foucault would have preferred that we not seek to explain his discourse by recourse to the incidents of his life, he would see the inevitability of our search. The fact that we can only understand Foucault according to the conventions of our time is one of the problems of which Foucault has made us aware. But even if we can do nothing other than to treat Foucault as an author, it should be kept in mind while reading the following pages that such treatment is conventional and historical, and not natural, for as Foucault more than anyone else has shown us, other periods and cultures have had different conventions of authorship.

Foucault's Career

Foucault was born in Poitiers in 1926, the son of a surgeon. He was an adolescent during the German occupation of France in World War II, an experience Foucault believes left a permanent mark: "I have very early memories of an absolutely threatening world which could crush us."[5] He was first enrolled in state schools in Poitiers, but later transferred to a Catholic school where he received his *baccalauréat* with distinction. He went to Paris in 1945 to prepare at the Lycée Henri IV for the entrance examination to the École Normale Supérieure (ENS). The ENS is one of the *grandes écoles* and as such, the most prestigious institution in France at which Foucault could have pursued a degree in liberal arts and sciences. Foucault entered the ENS and received the *licence* in both philosophy and psychology. In 1952 he was awarded an advanced degree, a diploma in psychopathology. Foucault's work in psychology accurately reflects his disenchantment with philosophy. Alan Sheridan reports that Foucault had long sought secret knowledge always promised at the next educational level; his studies in philosophy at the ENS taught him that there was no such secret knowledge.[6] After receiving his diploma, Foucault observed psychiatric practice as an intern at Ste. Anne mental hospital in Paris and taught courses in psychopathology at the Sorbonne. In 1954 he published his first book, *Maladie mentale et personnalité* (Mental illness and personality). Michael Clark calls this book "a modest study of various technical concepts in psychiatric theory," but he also notes that it includes a brief history of attitudes toward mental illness that would be expanded into *Histoire de la folie à l'âge classique* (*Madness and Civilization* is an abridged translation), his first important work.[7] In the meantime, Foucault left France to teach French at the University of Uppsala in Sweden. This act represents a disillusionment with psychiatric science as much as his turn to psychology had marked a reaction against philosophy. But it was also a more radical step since it meant that he was giving up the career in the French academy that his training at the ENS had promised. While in Sweden, and later in Warsaw and Hamburg where Foucault directed the French Institutes, he rethought both reason and science in terms of their histories. He stopped asking "What is Truth?," or "What is the surest path to Truth?," and asked instead "What is the hazardous career that Truth has followed?"[8] Foucault was not the first philosopher to make this turn to history; Friedrich Nietzsche and the Edmund Husserl of *The Crisis of European Sciences* had led the way. But both Nietzsche and Husserl remained at properly philosophical levels of abstraction, while Foucault began to look at the historical details of change in the history of psychiatry. The result was *Histoire de la folie à l'âge classique*, which Foucault presented in 1960 as his thesis for the *doctorat d'état*, the highest academic degree awarded in France. Since the thesis was not a traditional work of philosophy, the degree was awarded in history of science. Foucault returned to France in that year to become head of the philosophy department at the University of Clermont-Ferrand.

In 1961 *Histoire de la folie à l'âge classique* was published and received the Medal of the Centre National de la Recherche Scientifique. Though this award certainly indicates interest and approval on the part of some in the intellectual establishment in France, Foucault has said that the question he was posing here and later in *The Birth of the Clinic,* the question of relations between power and knowledge, "totally failed to interest those to whom I addressed it," that is, the French Left (*PK* 110). It failed, Foucault suggests, because of the political climate of that era in France. American readers may need to be reminded of the dominance of the Left in general and Marxism in particular in the intellectual scene in postwar France. Foucault himself had been a member of the Communist party during the late 1940s. Many other French intellectuals left the party in the 1950s, but unlike in the United States, they did not abandon their left-wing positions as a result of the revelations about Stalin's crimes. Thus Foucault joined Sartre, Barthes, and many others who were already or were about to become major figures on the independent French Left. Nevertheless, Foucault believes that the Communist party set the intellectual agenda until 1968. Its concerns were focused on gaining respectability and winning elections in France, and not on radically revising conceptions of knowledge or reforming the university. Hence, the Left found little of interest in *Histoire de la folie à l'âge classique* or *The Birth of the Clinic*.

While Foucault was at work on *The Birth of the Clinic,* he also completed and published a study of a protosurrealist writer, *Raymond Roussel.* This study demonstrates another aspect of Foucault's alienation from philosophy. Foucault's interest in literature and the arts was reflected in his choice of friends in the early fifties and in various ways in his historical and philosophical works that came later. Although it is common for European philosophers to be interested in the arts—Sartre after all wrote considerable fiction and literary criticism—Foucault's interest in literary modernism had a remarkable impact on his work. Although *Raymond Roussel* is Foucault's only book-length study of a writer, he later published a number of essays on literary figures including Georges Bataille, Maurice Blanchot, and Hölderlin, and a book on the painter René Magritte, *This is Not a Pipe.*

If *Histoire de la folie à l'âge classique* and *The Birth of the Clinic* met with less interest than he might have hoped, Foucault certainly must have been surprised by the overwhelming response to *The Order of Things* in 1966. The book sold out its initial printing of 3,000 in one week, and a second printing of 5,000 within six weeks. *The Order of Things* was the right book at the right time for several reasons. First, the book shared obvious affinities with then fashionable structuralism. Although this was even more true of *The Birth of the Clinic, The Order of Things* applied this structuralism to the broad sweep of intellectual history rather than to the narrow discussion of medicine in the eighteenth century. Second, and more important, *The Order of Things* scandalously attacked a cow sacred to most French intellectuals: man. Foucault proclaimed that it is no longer possible to think in our day other than in the void left by man's disappearance. Nietzsche, Foucault argued, showed that God's death meant man's disappearance, that the birth of superman meant the death of man.[9] By treating man not as a natural entity, an essence or ground, but as a construction of the discourse of the modern era, Foucault challenged the belief not just of conservative intellectuals, but of Marxists and many others on the Left as well, whose humanism depended upon a stable conception of human nature which the human sciences sought to elaborate.

Foucault's next book, *The Archaeology of Knowledge,* attempts to explain the method he had used in *Histoire de la folie à l'âge classique*, *The Birth of the Clinic*, and *The Order of Things*. But while Sheridan is undoubtedly correct in calling *The Archaeology* "an extended theoretical postscript to the earlier work"[10] in that *The Archaeology* makes little sense apart from those books, it also includes an almost wholly new set of terms. Unlike any other of Foucault's work, this one suffered from almost unrelieved abstraction. Where *The Order of Things* seemed daunting because of its range of reference, *The Archaeology* seemed to entrap one in an hermetic web of concepts connected only to each other. Needless to say, *The Archaeology* was not the success that Foucault's publishers had expected.

Thus it was undoubtedly *The Order of Things* that paved the way for Foucault's election to the Collège de France in 1970 as professor of the History of Systems of Thought. Still, it was a remarkable rise from the obscure, provincial institution at Clermont-Ferrand in 1960 and the new campus of the University of Paris at Vincennes— a ghetto for left-wing faculty and student troublemakers, where Foucault went in 1968—to France's most prestigious institution only two years later. In the interval between Clermont-Ferrand and Vincennes, Foucault also spent two years teaching in Tunis. It was at the end of this period that the May 1968 demonstrations occurred in France. But in spite of the fact the Foucault neither participated in nor even witnessed these demonstrations, they seem to have influenced him strongly. There is a marked shift in the preoccupations of the work he did after *The Archaeology of Knowledge*.

Faculty at the Collège de France teach no classes; their appointment requires them only to offer a series of public lectures. Foucault's inaugural lecture at the Collège was "The Discourse on Language," an essay that reflects his transition to his new emphasis on power and on institutions. While "The Discourse on Language" continues the preoccupation of *The Archaeology of Knowledge* with the rules that govern the production of discourse, these rules are now no longer understood as linguistic codes that generate a set of statements. Rather, "The Discourse on Language" deals with rules that govern the practice of discourse, that tell who is entitled to speak, that prohibit some discourses and marginalize others. These rules are not mysteriously imbedded deep in discourse, but are to be found by looking at the contexts and institutions in which discourse is spoken, such as hospitals and asylums or professions and disciplines. Another important transitional essay, "Nietzsche, Genealogy, History," was published in 1971. Here Foucault signals his increasing interest in power by identifying a new method for his investigations, "genealogy," taken from Nietzsche's *On the Genealogy of Morals,* a book that explains historical ideas of good and evil in terms of their advantages for the various social groups who advocated them. Where the earlier term "archaeology" had taken discourses as pure systems, Foucault now finds that discourses have uses and that history is the "endlessly repeated play of dominations."[11]

The first major work to result from this new orientation was *Discipline and Punish,* which appeared in 1975. It also reflected Foucault's renewed interest in social action that came in the wake of the May 1968 demonstrations. Foucault became active in an organization, known by the acronym GIP, that sought to provide prisoners with the means to speak for themselves about prison conditions and their other concerns. One result of Foucault's interest in prisons was *I, Pierre Rivière,* a collection of documents concerning a nineteenth-century parricide uncovered in the course of Foucault's research. Chief among the documents was the murderer's own narrative of his act. Bringing this material to light not only allowed a criminal to "speak" for himself, but also demonstrated Foucault's belief in the importance of such archival materials. In *Discipline and Punish,* Foucault returns to a focus on the rise of a major modern institution. He had already dealt with *The Birth of the Clinic* and had titled a chapter in *Histoire de la folie à l'âge classique,* the birth of the asylum. Now he takes up the birth of the prison. What is new about the approach of *Discipline and Punish,* however, is that the focus of the book is not on the prison itself, but rather on the "technologies" of organization and control that Foucault calls "discipline" and which are characteristic not only of the prison, but also of schools, factories, the military, and most other modern institutions. Foucault treats discipline as a new phenomenon that develops in the eighteenth century and becomes dominant in the nineteenth. As he traces the rise of discipline, Foucault is never content to remain at the level of theories of punishment, and what he produces as a result is a powerful new history of practice.

One year after *Discipline and Punish,* Foucault published the first volume of what was to be his last major project—it was left incomplete at his death in 1984—*The History of Sexuality. The History of Sexuality* had something of the same kind of impact that *The Order of Things* did when it proclaimed the disappearance of man. There were two such bombshells to be found in *The History of Sexuality*. The first was the treatment of sexuality not as some natural and fundamental human instinct or drive, but as yet another historical construct of discourse. The second was a repudiation of what Foucault calls the "repressive hypothesis," the belief that since the Victorian era Western humanity has continued to suffer as a result of its continued repression of sexuality. Foucault's counterclaim is that during this period sexuality was not silenced, but was instead the object of an explosion of discourse. At no time in history, Foucault suggests, has so much been said about sexuality. Foucault's original plan for *The History of Sexuality* was to cover the period he had dealt with before in other works, from the sixteenth century to the nineteenth. He discovered as he was researching this project, however, that he needed to go back further in history to discover why sexuality had become a moral experience. This led him ultimately to ancient Greece, which became the subject of volume 2, *The Uses of Pleasure*. Volume 3, *The Care of the Self*, published at the same time, dealt with ancient Rome. A fourth volume, *Les Aveux de la chair* (The confessions of the flesh), was left incomplete at Foucault's death. Foucault's research on sexuality also yielded an archival recovery, *Herculine Barbin: Being the Recently Discovered Memoirs of a Nineteenth-Century French Hermaphrodite*, which he edited and introduced.

Although *The History of Sexuality* may seem like a radical departure from *Discipline and Punish*, several ideas link them. The most striking connection is the preoccupation with power that is if anything even more pronounced in *The History of Sexuality*. In both studies Foucault was trying to work out a new way of thinking about power that recognized it as something productive as well as repressive. But Foucault himself drew a different link between the two books in 1982, when he argued that "it is not power, but the subject, which is the general theme of my research."[12] This was not the first time Foucault claimed such a broad coherence for his work. In an interview first published in 1976 entitled "Truth and Power," he claimed a similar role for power in his work beginning with *Madness and Civilization* (PK 115). Earlier still, in *Archaeology of Knowledge*, he claimed that the rules of discursive formation had been his subject all along. Each of these claims has some validity, but the very attempt to describe his work as a whole indicates that Foucault was thinking of himself as an author in that he was trying to assert that there were deeper continuities beneath the surface changes in his work. In the following chapters we will see how Foucault was correct in asserting these continuities in his oeuvre, but we will also attend to the contradictions and ruptures that led him to revise his overall characterization of it.

Chapter Two
Foucault's Strategies

Michel Foucault's work is difficult to understand not only because of its wide range of historical reference and its use of new concepts, but perhaps most of all because it does not fit very well into any of the established disciplines. Foucault, as I have said, was trained as a philosopher, but none of his books could be described as philosophy either in terms of continental or Anglo-American traditions. If Foucault's work were philosophical it could be treated as the articulation of a body of theory at minimum, and perhaps as a system. Furthermore, it is likely that this body of theory would provide answers to the questions that one or another philosophical school seeks to answer. Thus we might expect Foucault to address standard problems of metaphysics such as the mind/body problem, or of political philosophy, the problem of legitimacy, for example. Not only does Foucault avoid these traditional questions, but several commentators on Foucault have observed a lack of any theoretical positions in his work. Alan Sheridan calls him "profoundly anti-theoretical," and John Rajchman describes Foucault as a skeptic.[1] The lack of a system, or even a series of positions staked out on traditional issues, makes it impossible simply to write a straight-forward explanation of the content of Foucault's thought. Rather, it is necessary to find another approach to Foucault's body of work.

My approach in this chapter will focus on the strategies Foucault uses for understanding the past, works of art, systems of thought, and other "objects" with which he deals. This is especially appropriate because Foucault's own concerns are so often with strategies or things like them: techniques, technologies, etc. In using the term strategies, I am trying to emphasize the point that Foucault is not raising these approaches to the level of theoretical principles or truths. He is not saying that historians should always do x, or that discourse is always like y. Rather, the strategies are employed because they are useful for Foucault's ends under the conditions that he faces. This approach to Foucault is rhetorical in the sense that it attends to the way his discourse is constructed. Rhetoric here does not indicate form or style that can be separated from some more fundamental content or truth. Rather, just as Foucault's work assumes that truth cannot be separated from discourse or rhetoric, so I will regard Foucault's own discursive practices as indispensable to the ideas he articulates. Thus even though Foucault uses the term "principles" to describe what I call strategies, he means them to be methodological principles demanded by particular tasks he has set for himself. These tasks will be the subjects of the chapters that follow.

Foucault outlines his major strategies in "The Discourse on Language," which he introduces as a methodology required by the tasks or themes that will govern his work in the years to come. "The Discourse on Language" was written after the publication of *The Archaeology of Knowledge* (1969) and near the beginning of the long hiatus before the appearance of *Discipline and Punish* in 1975. In his inaugural lecture at the Collège de France it is not surprising that Foucault should be emphasizing his future work, but the strategies he names can apply equally well to his previous work. The four "principles" he mentions are reversal, discontinuity, specificity, and exteriority.[2] Each principle is in fact an approach Foucault had used before and would continue to use. These strategies are among the most consistent features of Foucault's corpus which otherwise covers an enormous range and contains much that is divergent.

Reversal

Reversal is the "master trope" of the four principles, the one that governs the other three, each of which are forms of reversal. Hayden White has argued that Foucault's work is characterized by a "reversed style," a description Foucault himself applied to Raymond Roussel. According to White, Foucault increasingly saw reversed style as a characteristic of all discourse.[3] In "The Discourse on Language," however, reversal is named as a strategy, as an action rather than a mere state. In the broadest sense, reversal means just what one might expect. When tradition gives us a particular interpretation of an event or an historical development, Foucault's strategy is to work out the implications of the reverse or opposite interpretation. The strategy of reversal tells Foucault what to look for by pointing to the simple existence of the other side of things. In "The Discourse on Language," Foucault says reversal seeks the negative activity of discourse where traditional philosophers and historians have been preoccupied with its positive role (*DC* 229). The strategy of reversal in its broadest usage leads us to discard the assumption that human thought—which Foucault calls discourse because thought is always expressed in a particular linguistic form—is at root rational and positive, that when it fails to be rational and positive it is merely an aberration, a departure from its true nature. Foucault assumes, for example, that those elements that seem to hold a discourse together, that guarantee its connection to some nondiscursive reality, cannot perform these functions without also performing negative ones that limit the discourse or rarefy it.

In chapter 1 we saw one of these principles of continuity at work: the notion of the author. When we consider the author-function, we are most likely to think of things that it does to make discourse more persuasive. When we attribute writing to an author we assume a continuity with the author's other writing. We assume that the author is speaking to us with some clear goal in mind. But Foucault's strategy is to reverse these assumptions of continuity and noncontradiction. In this case we look at the way attributing discourse to an author removes it from other connections it might have, and makes us overlook contradictions that might be there. Thus, by the strategy of reversal, we consider discourse as authorless.

The strategy of reversal can perhaps be seen more clearly if we look at Foucault's discussion of madness and psychiatry in *Madness and Civilization*. The traditional narrative about madness and its treatment is one of uninterrupted progress. As science developed, psychiatry became increasingly effective and humane. The mad used to be manacled and abandoned in institutions that, when they were not literally prisons, were no better than prisons; now they are treated just as the physically ill are treated. Foucault's reversal of this narrative is neither literal nor absolute. He is not saying that things have gone from good to bad. Rather, he looks for ways in which what has changed in the treatment of madness may not be for the best. He begins by discussing the practice during the late Middle Ages of sending the mad away on ships of fools. This practice suggests that the mad were not always subject to confinement and that the beginning of their confinement during the Renaissance resulted neither from humane nor scientific impulses, but from political and social needs that varied from nation to nation. In other words, to understand the history of madness, we do not look for some original object, madness in itself, to which all ideas of madness have ultimately aimed, but rather we must look at madness as a term or concept reinvented at different periods for different ends. This sort of reversal treats the name, rather than the thing or natural object, as the object of inquiry.

Another kind of reversal is the reversal of value. The traditional narrative of the development of the treatment of madness assumes a positive value. Foucault leads us to question this evaluation, not by showing that this or that particular therapy has failed to bring about a cure, but by pointing out the unintended and overlooked consequences of different forms of treatment. He points out, for example, that the mad whom Philippe Pinel released from their chains after the French Revolution became in some respects less free because now they were no longer able to simply be mad. For "the free terror of madness" was substituted "the stifling anguish of responsibility. . . . The asylum no longer punished the madman's guilt, it is true, but it did more, it organized that guilt."[4] Foucault's reversal here produces a strange new picture of the history of the treatment of the mad. The act that for so long was depicted as an act of liberation, a humanitarian realization that the mad were not guilty and should not therefore be imprisoned like criminals, is now shown to be an exchange of one form of unfreedom for another, perhaps less physically cruel, but more intrusive and powerful in its effects on the patient's life.

Foucault's other books that focus on major institutions—*Birth of the Clinic, Discipline and Punish*—also present reversals of the usual historical evaluation of the development of the hospital and the prison. Perhaps Foucault's most striking historical reversal, however, is his critique of the "repressive hypothesis" in the first volume of *The History of Sexuality*.[5] The repressive hypothesis holds that since the Victorian era civilization has continued to repress human sexuality in spite of our best efforts to free ourselves from this repression. We are told that sex remains a dark secret stifled by social and self-censorship, and finds all sorts of disguised means to express itself. Foucault argues that this entire reading of the history of modern sexuality is mistaken. In fact, says Foucault, rather than being an unspoken secret, sexuality has been during the twentieth century a topic of prolific conversation. Such discourse has not, however, secured us a liberation from Victorian silence—a silence that Foucault acknowledges—but rather the creation of "sexuality" itself. Like madness, sexuality turns out not to be a natural human state or drive, but rather a discourse, a way of talking and hence a way of thinking. But in saying "a way" we must be careful not to infer the idea that it is one among many ways we can choose. Rather, sexuality is the discourse in which we come to experience. There can be no access to some pure experience of sex apart from the discourse of sexuality. Foucault reverses the hypothesis of repressive silence and presents us with a picture of sex under the imperative to speak.

We have thus seen the strategy of reversal at work on what we might call several different levels of discourse. At the most general level, Foucault looks for the negative side of the statements that make up the discourses he studies, discourses about madness, medicine, penology, sexuality, etc. At this level, reversal pertains to conditions of all discourses in the sense that all discourses make positive statements, and there are always negative consequences of any positive statement. This level provides the theoretical justification for carrying out the strategy to examine the content of discursive systems. Thus, on another level, Foucault also uses the strategy of reversal on the major claims of particular discourses, such as the claim of sexuality to be silenced by repression. It is true that these reversals of major claims are only sustainable on the basis of a more general pattern of reversal, but it is not clear where the process begins. Foucault may be as likely to begin by saying "What if we looked at the vast total discourse about sex rather than the single claim that sex is repressed?," as to begin by saying "What is the negative side of sexuality as a discourse?"

Discontinuity

I have already alluded to the strategy of discontinuity in noting that continuity is one of the basic, positive assumptions of discourse. We tend to assume continuity is everywhere: in authors' oeuvres; in the historical development of a contemporary object or state of affairs; in the relationship between thought or language, on the one hand, and the world or reality they represent, on the other. Foucault's "discontinuous" view of history is, perhaps, the idea for which he is most famous. In my discussion of *The Order of Things* I will find occasion to take up in greater detail Foucault's remark that he is "flabbergasted" by the notion that he has founded his theory of history on discontinuity (*PK* 111). Here it will suffice to observe that to *found* a theory of history on discontinuity would be to think in terms of a foundation, a continuity. Nonetheless, Foucault does treat history as if it were discontinuous. That is, he looks for ruptures, breaks, gaps, displacements, mutations, shifts, interruptions, thresholds, etc. The variety of terms listed here, all of them used in *The Archaeology of Knowledge,* suggests the importance of discontinuities in Foucault's thinking. It is perhaps the major instance of reversal in his work.

To understand the importance of the strategy of discontinuity, we need to understand more about the assumption of continuity. Two major metaphors are commonly used to describe historical time: the arrow and the cycle.[6] Both imply continuity, although of different kinds. The cycle implies a continuous pattern of changes, but the same changes are endlessly repeated. While the end of one cycle and the beginning of the next may be depicted as cataclysmic, no real change occurs since the result of the cataclysm is merely the return of the same. The arrow is the more powerful of the two metaphors in modern Western thought, and it allows for even less discontinuity than the cycle. The arrow is the root metaphor for the notion of progress, the gradual, evolutionary improvement of the world during the course of history. The effect of this view of history is to render the present as always better than any past period, and also to project a still better period to come. The root of this view of history is the Hebrew Bible, and its dominance occurred as a result of the triumph of Christianity in Europe. Modern secular theories of history such as those of Herbert Spencer and Karl Marx derive from this theological root. The belief in progress renders each moment, each event significant since nothing is ultimately irrelevant to the creation of the future. Thus, the doctrine of progress carries with it a kind of secular providence that renders everything continuous with everything else. But the arrow metaphor has become even stronger in the modern era because it has come to dominate the conception of time in geology—under the name gradualism—and in biology, from which science we now appropriate the term "evolution" for use in connection with all facets of human history. The gradualist view of history holds that major changes occur as the result of the accumulation of many smaller changes, not as major cataclysms or catastrophes. Thus we understand the past not only as moving in the direction of a positive future, but moving there gradually, continuously, without major breaks or gaps.

In the face of these assumptions of continuity, Foucault asks not that we assume precisely the opposite—that there is no continuity in history—but rather that we treat any assumed continuity with suspicion. Furthermore, he suggests that instead of looking *always* for continuities, that we look for discontinuities, which he names ruptures, thresholds, etc. This in itself would not make Foucault an unusual historian, since history is typically preoccupied with "events," that is, with the moments where the normal course of things is interrupted, where major changes occur. But it has been the preoccupation of history to *explain* these changes. Such explanation requires underlying continuities that we might think of as "historical laws." For example, in American history, the Civil War is usually treated as a kind of rupture. Our word for describing the country before the war, *antebellum,* conveys a sense of radical difference before and after the war. But to explain the Civil War and the changes it brought about, we need to assume that events such as wars obey certain regularities, that, for example, two widely divergent social and economic formations under the same government will inevitably come into conflict. But it is precisely these sorts of continuities that Foucault does not wish to rely upon. As a result, his own histories do not discuss the causes for the ruptures he indicates.

It is this absence of causal explanation that makes Foucault's view of history seem so radically discontinuous. Many of his books present us with several different periods of history and focus on the differences in a given field of thought and practice during each period. The clearest and most famous example of this procedure occurs in *The Order of Things,* where Foucault invokes his concept of the *episteme* to describe the intellectual conditions of possibility during the Renaissance, the classical age (by which Foucault means 1650–1800), and the modern era. Foucault describes vastly different conditions during each period, but offers no hint as to why each began or ended. Foucault's strategy of discontinuity is perhaps most shocking in this work because its scope is so broad. Foucault appears to be saying that the whole world changes, almost overnight, in 1650 and again in 1800, but he does not tell us why. As we will see later, Foucault's claims are much more modest than this since he does not regard the *episteme* as the foundation for the world, but only of certain discourses about it. Nevertheless, his strategy is deeply disconcerting because it violates our assumptions of historical continuity. But the strategy of discontinuity allows Foucault to concentrate on the structure of each period and to emphasize the radical character of its differences from the others. Paradoxically, it also helps him to point out what is similar in patterns that, changing only the arrangement of their elements, repeat themselves from one *episteme* to the next.

Specificity

This leads us to consider the third strategy, the assumption of the specificity of particular discourses or historical formations. This strategy begins with the reversal of our common assumption that discourse is a more or less accurate representation of a nondiscursive reality. Foucault begins rather with the assumption that discourse is a violence that we do to things, a practice we impose on them. The world itself is not assumed to have its own expression, which we can translate into our own language. Madness, for example, cannot be understood apart from some particular discourse. That is why we cannot write the history of psychiatry as the changing methods of treating or otherwise dealing with a definite phenomenon characterized always by the same patterns of behavior. Madness is something different in each specific discourse, in spite of whatever behavioral consistencies might be discovered among its representations in different historical periods. Historians of science have traditionally ignored this problem by assuming that each discourse was intended as a step toward the discovery of the truth that the present scientific community accepts. Thus past discourses are not presented in their specificity, but as part of one great, transcendental conversation that has led inevitably to where we are today. Foucault insists, on the other hand, that we take seriously what earlier discourses were trying to do, that we attend to the features that distinguish these discourses from each other and from our own.

Yet Foucault cannot approach this problem in a straightforward way. If he were to simply spell out the difference between a modern conception of madness and a Renaissance one, he would risk rendering the earlier one in terms of the present one. The very activity of comparison—especially where one of the things compared carries the weight of truth, while the other is known to have been discarded as false by history—will compromise the specificity of the historical object. Foucault's answer to this dilemma is to immerse the reader in the discourse he is discussing. This method is revealed quite strikingly in *The Order of Things* where Foucault goes on for pages without reminding the reader that he is discussing the perspective of the Renaissance or the classical age. If one fails to keep the historical frame of reference in mind, one will find oneself attempting to make sense of bizarre but seemingly carefully constructed arguments that Foucault himself is advancing. It may seem, for example, that Foucault is arguing that things bear resemblances to each other that can be deciphered by clever readers to reveal the truth of the world, when in fact Foucault is merely trying to demonstrate how the Renaissance *episteme* worked. But he does this often without comparison, and for long stretches without reminding the reader that he is talking about a distant historical period. The strategy here is to make you experience that period's discourse as a specific self-sufficient web that can account for the whole of its own world. While the history of science typically shows us failures, Foucault's strategy attempts to give us a sense of the earlier *episteme* as a perfectly complete and convincing mode of gaining knowledge.

The strategy of specificity might thus also be called the strategy of "alterity," or otherness. Foucault asks us to assume that historical periods prior to the modern era are radically different from our own. He eschews any considerations of human nature or other grounds for assuming the transhistorical similarity of human beings. This, of course, follows from the assumption of discontinuity, but it is not the same assumption. Discontinuity says that we will look for ruptures of the typical continuity of history. The strategy of alterity says that we should assume that the objects or periods divided by these ruptures are radically different. Thus, another reason for Foucault's deliberate method of not reminding the reader of the historical frame of reference for ideas he is discussing is that not doing so causes the reader to experience more strongly their strangeness. This feeling is particularly striking in Foucault's discussion of the Renaissance *episteme* where we feel entirely immersed in an utterly alien way of thought. Yet the difficulty that readers new to Foucault have in recognizing that he is not advocating this way of thinking suggests the success of Foucault's rhetoric but may seem to undermine his claims for the radical alterity of this perspective. If it were so unthinkable in the twentieth century, why would anyone attribute it to Foucault? The answer may be that Foucault is dealing at a level of thought in *The Order of Things,* which is itself alien to most readers.

Exteriority

The fourth strategy, exteriority, is yet another reversal of modern intellectual convention, which has sought through a variety of means and in differing systems of thought to discover the meaning of discourse in depths that the surface meaning disguises. This search for deep meaning has characterized psychoanalysis and Marxism, and also much literary criticism of the twentieth century. Foucault calls the kind of interpretation that seeks deep meaning "commentary," and he regards it as an example of the belief that there is a legible reality outside of discourse (*BC* xvi). To look at the exterior of discourse is to treat it as unmotivated or unintentional, rather than to attempt to discover a rational or irrational cause. Freudian psychoanalysis would seek to explain a particular feature of a text— a literary work, a dream, neurotic behavior—as a symptom of some deeper psychological reality, especially sexual desire. A more traditional form of literary criticism might seek to discover the expression of moral good or evil in poems or novels. In each case, the surface text is supposed to point to a more fundamental reality. Foucault wants to take the surface of discourse itself as the fundamental reality.

But by the surface of discourse, Foucault does not mean style or form in any of their usual senses. Foucault continues to be concerned with the semantic aspect of language even though he rejects the search for meaning as it has traditionally been conceived. Foucault's strategy of exteriority is to look for the "conditions of existence" of discourse, "for that which gives rise to the chance series of these events and fixes its limits" (*DC* 229). The conditions of existence come in two varieties. The first is a function of the discourse itself. Foucault argues that within any system of discourse only certain statements are possible. To describe the conditions of existence of a discourse at this level is to seek to understand the range of possible statements that the discourse can produce. Foucault gives the name *archaeology* to this project. On another level, however, the conditions of existence of a discourse are external to it in the sense that they are social conditions. Such conditions include how the right to speak is governed within a discourse, or when it is appropriate to speak in this discourse. These conditions are governed by the role the discourse plays in the relations of power in a society. Foucault will use the word *genealogy* to describe this approach to the conditions of discourse. What makes discourse a "chance series of events" is that both the structural limits and the social conditions of discourse combine to produce statements such that the goals or motives of individual speakers become irrelevant to Foucault's analysis. Rather, Foucault's strategy of exteriority leads him to imagine the production of discourse as something like a dice game. His job is not to guess why seven or eleven came up on a particular roll, but rather to establish what numbers are on the dice and of what use a seven or eleven might be to particular players in the game.

Perhaps the best example of the archaeological approach to the exterior of discourse comes from *The Order of Things,* where Foucault produces a four-term set of oppositions whose changed relationships mark the difference between the *episteme* of the classical age and that of the modern era illustrated by a diagram called the General Table, or quadrilateral, diagrammed in chapter 4. It is the perfect example of the strategy of exteriority because it is not a successful visual aid for explaining Foucault's ideas. It succeeds more in showing the kind of thinking Foucault does rather than at elucidating the particular analyses and concepts he presents. The key terms— *articulation, attribution, designation, derivation*—come from the classical project of a general grammar, but they are seen as representing the different possibilities open under each *episteme.* The diagram in chapter 4 shows that the sciences characteristic of each *episteme* contain an element corresponding to each of four terms. The *episteme* in the broadest sense is defined by the relations of these terms, while each science is defined by the relations of the corresponding elements. Thus, even though there were differences among general grammarians, among natural historians, among analysts of wealth— the names of these sciences are unfamiliar because Foucault wants to distinguish classical age sciences from their modern equivalents, linguistics, biology, and political economy—in each case the differences are all contained within the elements of the quadrilateral that represents the conditions enabling the opposing systems to be thought.

Explanation of the argument that the diagram is intended to

support must await the detailed discussion of *The Order of Things* in chapter 4, but I can say here that Foucault is arguing that purely formal or structural conditions define what may be said within a broad group of sciences during a given period. This argument ex-emplifies exteriority because it ignores both what the practitioners of these sciences would have said about their own assumptions and because it does not seek some transhistorical truth that the discourses of these sciences systematically mask. Instead, Foucault finds a kind of grid or map of options that is both purely arbitrary in that it is not designed or produced out of the interests of any class or group *and* absolutely inclusive, since to speak in terms other than those provided on the grid would be to do something other than the science in question. That is, Foucault does not deny that people could think in terms other than the ones specified on the quadri-lateral, but if they did they would not be recognized as natural historians, general grammarians, or analysts of wealth.

The genealogical version of exteriority is perhaps best illustrated by Foucault's history of the changing means of social retribution and control—torture, punishment, and discipline—in *Discipline and Punish*. These different juridical practices are not pictured as being produced by different conditions of discourse as the human sciences are pictured in *The Order of Things*. Nor, however, are they depicted as stemming from more fundamental economic or political changes as a Marxist analysis might insist. That is to say, as in the archae-ological approach, there is no deep truth that genealogical analysis is designed to reveal. But genealogy does differ from archaeology precisely because political and economic concerns are taken into account. It now becomes very much to the point of Foucault's thinking to observe that some social groups benefit from these changes and that each works hand in glove with the social system dominant during its period. In the genealogical approach, Foucault remains concerned with the limits and conditions of discourse, but he no longer understands these limits and conditions as linguistic.

While Foucault has all along treated discourse as more than mere language, in the genealogical approach he emphasizes the fact that discourses are always "discursive practices," that discourse always exists in the context of a specific institutional environment. Thus in *Discipline and Punish,* although Foucault does analyze discourse about each system, torture, punishment, and discipline are primarily treated as practices or technologies. By attending to the surface of these practices, Foucault can focus on what has been called micro-power, the relations of power within institutions, as opposed to macropower, the relations of power between institutions or classes, which has been the traditional concern of political science. The strategy of exteriority in this case leads Foucault to notice different events and different conditions of possibility for those events than historians have typically observed. He is able to do this because he takes seriously the features of the practice of torture or of discipline, where others have tended to look past those features to some deeper truth conceived in advance.

This last observation may lead one to conceive of the strategy of exteriority as a kind of empiricism. Although Foucault may himself be something of an empiricist or even a positivist, he is neither of these in any usual sense. To be an empiricist, Foucault would have to believe that some kind of theory-less perception of the world were possible. Nothing could be further from Foucault's position. Rather, Foucault believes that all looking is conditioned by pre-conceptions, by discourse, by the habits he calls "practices." The strategy of exteriority does not stem from a claim about the true being plain and visible, but from a rejection of the claim that the true is systematically disguised. Nevertheless, there is in exteriority a connection to the old theme in Western thought of looking at or returning to "the things themselves" rather than continuing to assert our assumptions about things. What is radical about Foucault's strategy is the kinds of things he looks at. Foucault's discussion of "discipline," for example, involves the creation of a new concept that unites techniques of military training, education, penology, and manufacturing—among others—as aspects of a new regime of social organization and control. The discovery of this concept of discipline could not have occurred so long as one continued to see all of these techniques as the effects of economic determinations or political theories, but it also could not have occurred without the theory of micropower that develops out of the analysis of medicine in *The Birth of the Clinic*. Exteriority, like the other strategies I have discussed here, is thus aimed at overthrowing other habits of mind rather than at establishing a new basis of truth.

Chapter Three
Madness and the Gaze

Although Michel Foucault is often experienced as a difficult writer, let it never be assumed that this is the result of his inattention to matters of style and rhetorical effect. An indication of his attention to rhetoric is to be found in the startling beginnings of so many of his books. One characteristic ploy is to begin with an explicit reversal of some assumption or belief we take for granted. *Madness and Civilization* begins twice by invoking a reversal. The "Preface" quotes Pascal: "Men are so necessarily mad, that not to be mad would amount to another form of madness" (*MC* ix). This quotation immediately causes the reader to question any simple division of the sane and insane that he or she had been carrying about. This questioning should be disorienting to many, since being able to distinguish the mad from the rest of us is something upon which we depend both for our faith in the knowledge of professionals such as psychiatrists and our confidence in our own mental health. But it is essential to Foucault's purpose in *Madness and Civilization* that the reader be disoriented, for Foucault wants us to understand madness itself as an arbitrary classification created during the historical period he will discuss in the book. His task will be to return to "that zero point in the course of madness at which madness is an undifferentiated experience. . . . This is doubtless an uncomfortable region. To explore it we must renounce the convenience of terminal truths, and never let ourselves be guided by what we may know of madness" (*MC* ix). Foucault's attempt at disorienting the reader is designed to permit this renunciation to occur; it is never easy—Foucault might argue that it is finally impossible—to bracket what one already knows.

The History of Madness

The second startling beginning is the opening sentence of the first chapter: "At the end of the Middle Ages, leprosy disappeared from the Western world" (*MC* 3). At the level of medical science,

27

this statement is technically false. Leprosy did not at the end of the
Middle Ages go the way of small pox in the twentieth century.
There was, it is true, what Foucault calls the regression of the disease,
which he notes occurred not because of the success of obscure medical
practices but of confinement itself and the end of the Crusades,
which meant a break in the link with the sources of the infection.
But we do not get this information for several pages. Foucault's
failure to qualify the statement at the outset is one of the things
that makes it so effective. What we want is a qualification indicating
that Foucault was not talking about the disease as a medical problem,
but as a social phenomenon whose interest to him we might be
tempted to call symbolic—such a qualification would clarify things
for the reader. But it would also establish dependence upon an
epistemological system Foucault wants to undermine. Foucault does
not want us to rely on our faith in modern science to always tell us
the truth. He wants us to experience the past not by constant
reference to the present, but in its ineluctable otherness. Thus Foucault gives us a historical event in unfamiliar terms. But these terms
are not those that the people at the turn of the century would have
found familiar either. We would be wrong to imagine someone in
the late Middle Ages coming home after a consultation with other
leaders and saying to his wife, "Guess what? Leprosy has disappeared." Foucault shows this himself when he notes that leprosariums continued to exist in France as late as 1695, well into the
classical age. It is true that in 1635 the people of Reims actually
celebrated a solemn procession to thank God for delivering them
from the disease, but for Europe as a whole, the disappearance of
leprosy took more than three centuries.

Leprosy's disappearance is an important event to Foucault because
it marks a shift in the grounds for confinement and in the people
whom society found appropriate to marginalize and control in this
way. As the leprosariums emptied of lepers, they started to be used
for other purposes, for other confinements. It will not surprise us
to learn that the mad will be among those who will replace the
lepers. But we may be surprised when told that leprosy was not
merely a medical issue, that confinement of lepers was a good deal
more than a simple quarantine. What would outlast the leprosariums
"were the values and images attached to the figure of the leper as
well as the meaning of his exclusion, the social importance of that
insistent and fearful figure which was not driven off without first

being inscribed within a sacred circle" (*MC* 6). The leper's exclusion from society was a kind of guarantee of his salvation as a witness to the world's evil. Thus lepers, as will vagabonds, criminals, and the insane of a later period, find their own salvation assured by their exclusion. Foucault argues that the forms of exclusion of the Middle Ages persist into the very different culture of the Renaissance still associated with spiritual renewal.

Madness/Folly in the Renaissance. Having established both a thematic continuity—the spiritual value of exclusion—and a historical discontinuity—the disappearance of leprosy—Foucault goes on to describe the way madness is depicted in Renaissance literary and visual arts. Foucault's use of artistic representations may seem surprising since he simply assumes that they are representative of commonly held beliefs. As we will discover, literature and painting will figure importantly in several other of Foucault's books, but the use will differ in these later works. *Madness and Civilization* uses artistic works in a way that is similar to that of American intellectual historians such as Barbara Novak or Henry Nash Smith. Art is not a privileged window into cultural or intellectual life of the period in the sense that it presents a prophetic or more profound view. Rather it is the major evidence Foucault has for the picture of madness in the Renaissance he presents. This is one clue that the "commentary" that Foucault will specifically eschew in the preface to *The Birth of the Clinic* is very much a part of Foucault's argument in *Madness and Civilization*.

What Foucault discovers in the literature and art of the Renaissance is that madness is not silent, that it is given voice within culture even though madness, like leprosy, is considered evil and cause for expulsion or confinement. Sebastian Brant's poem, *Narrenschiff* (Ship of fools), and Hieronymus Bosch's painting, *Ship of Fools,* which seems to illustrate a canto of Brant's poem, anticipate in their differences the "great line of cleavage in the Western experience of madness" (*MC* 18). Foucault argues that in the visual arts the breakdown of the great Gothic symbolism of the Middle Ages freed the image "from wisdom and from the teaching that organized it" and left it to "gravitate about its own madness" (*MC* 18). Paintings and drawings present scenes that approach the condition of dreams. Like the dream, the visual image no longer teaches, but fascinates.

Foucault calls special attention to gryllos, grotesques created in the Middle Ages to illustrate the imprisonment of humans by desire. A gryllos is, according to Foucault, an image of human madness, madness here being defined as being consumed by desire, as spirit corrupted by the folly of sin. In the Renaissance these "hermetic, demented forms" become the visual language of numerous *temptations*, paintings that depict the ordeals of saints. Rather than being confronted by the objects of desire—food or flesh or money—the saint faces these strange dream creatures usually showing a human face conjoined to an animal body. Looking at paintings such as Bosch's *The Temptation of Saint Anthony*, one can easily see Foucault's point. This large triptych certainly could be understood to convey a conventional message about the power of temptation, but such a message does not hit one over the head. Instead, the eye is drawn to one and then another strange image that call attention more to themselves than to the meaning of the work as a whole. The gryllos that stares at the saint is characterized by Foucault as an image of madness become temptation itself, or, to put it another way, the gryllos is both subject and object of temptation, both an image of the desirer and an image of what is desired. The ascetic no longer desires things of the flesh but instead his own hallucinations.

The fools in Bosch's *Ship of Fools* are, like the gryllos, images of madness. In each case, the fool conveys a kind of wisdom that is the knowledge of the limits of wisdom, of the fact of forbidden knowledge. The tree of knowledge, for example, serves as the mast of Bosch's *Ship of Fools*. The point Foucault wants to make about all of this is that madness had something to tell the Renaissance world. It had a function then as did leprosy: to testify to the reality of sin. These images of madness anticipate the apocalypse and predict a "world where all wisdom is annihilated. . . . The end has no value as passage and promise; it is the advent of a night in which the world's old reason is engulfed" (MC 23). Thus reason and madness speak with distinct voices, with madness having the last word. Several writers of the Renaissance produced work consistent with this general pattern, most notably Cervantes and Shakespeare. "Doubtless, both testify more to a tragic experience of madness appearing in the fifteenth century, than to a critical and moral experience of Unreason developing in their own epoch" (MC 31). Like the painters, Cervantes and Shakespeare depict madness as an extreme place in that it is beyond appeal, where nothing can ever restore it to reason or truth, and from whence nothing can come except laceration and death (*MC* 31). Lady MacBeth's doctor calls her madness "disease beyond my practice." Even when Don Quixote seems to regain his reason in the moments before his death, we do not know whether this is merely another form of madness.

In the literature typical of the Renaissance, however, Foucault contends that madness is not a prediction of the end of reason. Rather, madness is associated with frivolousness, with making people joyous and playful. Folly reigns not only over what is bad in humanity, but also indirectly over the good of which it is capable. Human good has its roots in the same desires as evil. Ambition creates wise leaders; avarice causes wealth to grow. It is true that the literary depiction of madness also associated it with knowledge, but not because madness controls knowledge. Rather knowledge that does not address itself to experience is depicted as folly, as an excess of learning. Thus Erasmus in *In Praise of Folly* finds madness in everyone in the form of inflated self-regard and rampant illusions. Literary and philosophical treatments of madness take the form of moral satire, and madness most often manifests itself in the gentle irony of its illusions. It is this moral and critical view of madness that Brant's *Narrenschiff* anticipates.

In the Renaissance madness appears as an enormously complex experience. The mad are recognized as part of the world, but like lepers are often excluded from society. While such exclusion sometimes took the form of confinement—there were places of detention reserved for the insane during the Middle Ages—the ship of fools is most characteristic. These ships actually existed and provided a way to assure permanent exile of those expelled. Although they do not represent freedom in any simple sense, they are in some respect the opposite of the hospital, since rather than being confined, the mad are forced to wander. The exclusion of the mad involves elements of ritual purification of the community, but the mad voyagers also exemplify the borderline position that the mad occupied in Renaissance society. "It is for the other world that the madman sets sail in his fools' boat; it is from the other world that he comes when he disembarks" (*MC* 11). So the practice of expelling the mad by boat represents the role madness plays as an ever-present border beyond which reason cannot go, but which foretells the coming of apocalypse as the abolition of human reason. Yet at the same time a contrary conception of madness emerged that pointed not to evil and death, but to error and illusion. This moral and critical treatment of madness will lead to the birth of a new "madness" in the classical age.

Madness in the Age of Reason. This discussion of madness in the art and literature of the Renaissance is followed by a shift in focus when Foucault takes up the classical age. Instead of performing similar readings of the representation of madness in cultural production, Foucault deals with government policies, conditions of confinement, taxonomies of mental disease, etc. His discussion of the Renaissance has provided a background against which the specific characteristics of madness in the classical age will stand out. "Madness," it must now be emphasized, does not refer to a particular group of diseases that have existed throughout history while we have slowly but surely come to understand their true natures and causes. Rather, "madness" is a concept the meaning of which changes in spite of the fact that certain similar behaviors are continually identified with it. Our habit in trying to understand the past is to use *our* categories as if they were the dimly understood goals of earlier thinkers. Foucault wants to insist on the radical difference of madness in each of the three periods he will discuss: the Renaissance, the classical age, and the modern period or nineteenth century. Thus, for example, Foucault will insist that there was no psychology until the end of the eighteenth century when the asylum was born, because the classical age conceived of body and soul as connected strongly enough to preclude the notion of a nonphysical disease. The discussion of the classical age in *Madness and Civilization* will show that madness had many definitions during the period—some of them contradictory—but none of these conceptualizations represent progress toward psychology.

If the ship symbolized madness during the Renaissance, the hospital is its characteristic representation during the Age of Reason. "By a strange act of force, the classical age was to reduce to silence the madness whose voices the Renaissance had just liberated, but whose violence it had already tamed" (*MC* 38). The beginning of this period in the history of madness Foucault marks with the date of the decree that founded the Hôpital Général in Paris: 1656. This institution was not intended to function medically. Rather, it was something like a prison—it had irons and dungeons—and its inmates included not only the mad but also the poor, vagrants, common criminals, and others who were deemed dangerous to society. The Hôpital Général had authority independent of the police and the courts to confine individuals without appeal. The establishment of the Hôpital Général in Paris was the administrative beginning of "the great confinement," a massive social program in which one of every one hundred Parisians was confined in the Hôpital Général. Similar institutions were soon established throughout France. And the practice of confinement did not stop at the French border; throughout Europe during this period, confinement became increasingly important as a strategy to deal with undesirable people of all descriptions. Houses of correction began to be used in Germany and Switzerland even before the Paris decree. In England, the use of workhouses dates from the 1690s. By the end of the eighteenth century, institutions of confinement were so widespread in Europe that John Howard traveled to six countries to investigate the phenomenon.

Foucault argues that the origins of the great confinement lie in a fear of idleness. What all of the inmates of these institutions shared in spite of their great differences was their failure to work. There had been numerous attempts to rid cities of beggars and the unemployed since the sixteenth century. The edict of 1657 was the last of these measures and, in addition to creating an institution for confinement, it also made begging illegal in Paris and its suburbs. There were economic motives for the confinement. Crises caused large numbers of unemployed who were regarded as threats to social stability and who were duly rounded up and confined. But since the inmates in these institutions were invariably made to work, the institutions of confinement were, during periods of low unemployment, supposed to keep wages low by providing a low-cost labor force. Foucault argues, however, that these economic motives do not really explain either the confinement itself or the insistence on labor at these institutions, for, as methods of production, they failed. Instead, labor was regarded as a sacred imperative by both Protestant and Catholic theologians, and idleness was understood as a rebellion against God, a way of tempting him to provide by means of miracles. The requirement of labor in the houses of confinement was an exercise in moral reform and constraint. The institutions of the monarchy administered the bourgeois idea that virtue is an affair of the state. Rather than finding their ultimate justification in economics, the houses of confinement administered morality like a trade or commodity. Foucault concludes that in the seventeenth century madness was first understood in terms of poverty, the inability to work, and the failure to integrate with a group, and thus came to be classified among the problems of the modern city. No longer the visible representation of the limits of reason, madness became "sequestered and, in the fortress of confinement, bound to Reason" (MC 64).

After explaining the great confinement, Foucault proceeds to describe the explanations for the confinement of the mad and the conditions under which they in particular were kept. Even though madness was considered a form of idleness and the mad were confined together with all manner of other idle people, madness did not loose its distinct identity. That identity, however, was not as a representation of another world, nor as an illness as we are inclined to think today. If madness in the Renaissance represented Evil, the work of the devil, in the classical age it represented nothing except itself. It was not even the sign of a disease, since mad people were not understood to be sick, but to have on the contrary an animal strength that allowed them to endure conditions that other humans could not tolerate. The insane were often housed under conditions of extreme cold with little or nothing in the way of clothing to protect them. The insane of the classical age were regarded as animals, that is, as humans who have lost their reason leaving only their animal nature. Like animals, they were put on display to members of the public who could come to the institution to watch the mad, just as people might go to a zoo to watch exotic animals. According to Foucault, "madness was less than ever linked to medicine; nor could it be linked to the domain of correction. Unchained animality could be mastered only by *discipline* and *brutalizing*" (MC 75, italics in original). Animality here was not the realm of mechanistic processes that we might infer from classical science and thus it did not carry with it the deterministic implications that modern thought often gives to it. Rather the animal nature was a realm of anarchic freedom, of unreason. Madness was the empirical form of an underlying unreason that threatened to swallow up reason.

Foucault next describes the explanations the classical age gave for madness itself. Although the classical age did not treat madness as the result of deterministic animal drives, it did have a whole mechanics of madness which has its origin in the passions. But passion is not—or not merely—one of the causes of madness. For the classical age, "the possibility of madness is . . . implicit in the very phenomenon of passion" (MC 88). Prior to this period, going back to Greek and Roman antiquity, madness had been understood as punishment for passion's excesses, and passion was understood as temporary madness. But the classical age reversed this relation by treating madness as a form of passion. Passion was regarded as having its location in neither body nor soul, but both, and madness therefore was considered as a disease of both, although one which threatened their unity. Passion was regarded as literal movement within the person which could lead to madness in two ways: either the movement could become so excessive that it cancels itself out and produces immobility, where the person "resembles a statute more than a living being" (*MC* 90); or, the movement continues indefinitely, beginning with slight agitation from outside, but growing until it results in convulsions. By either route, the passions cause a derangement of the imagination that produces more than the mere unreason of passion itself, but the unreal, or the nothingness of madness.

This unreality is characterized by the belief in something merely imagined. To imagine that I am dead is not madness since I qualify the image precisely as something only imagined. But if I affirm, "I am dead," giving my statement value as truth, that is madness. The mad are not incapable of logic; in fact, they often manifest a rigorous logic as in the following syllogism: "The dead do not eat; I am dead; hence I do not eat" (*MC* 95). Madness is a form of error, of believing with confidence and conviction what is false. The mad person deceives himself. And how does he deceive himself? His reason is dazzled: "To say that madness is dazzlement is to say that the madman sees the daylight . . . as the man of reason (both live in the same brightness); but seeing this same daylight, and . . . nothing in it, he sees it as a void, as night, as nothing. . . . Which means that . . . he does not see at all. And believing he sees, he admits as realities the hallucinations of his imagination" (*MC* 108). Thus delirium and dazzlement are the essence of madness, just as truth and light are the essence of classical reason. Confinement is appropriate to madness so conceived because confinement acknowledges that madness is nothing.

Madness was not understood as a unitary phenomenon, but as having the differing forms of mania, melancholia, hysteria, and hypochondria. What is significant about the ways the classical age dealt with mania and melancholia is that they are not psychological and they do not stem from observation. Thus Foucault argues that

Thomas Willis, who is regarded as having discovered the characteristic alternation of mania and melancholia, did not treat this
pattern as an observed phenomenon in need of explanation, but as
a consequence of the predisposition of each to have a natural affinity
for the other. Instead of moving from observation to explanatory
image, the classical age began with images of such oppositions as
movement and immobility or fire and smoke that organized its
perceptions.

Discussions of hysteria and hypochondria were not based on observation either. Unlike mania and melancholia, this pair never came
to be understood as having a coherent group of qualities, and they
were not even regarded as forms of madness until the latter part of
the eighteenth century. Hysteria, prior to the seventeenth century,
was believed to be caused by the spontaneous movement of the
womb throughout a woman's body. Although seventeenth-century
physicians eventually recognized the womb as fixed in its location,
until the end of the eighteenth century the womb continued to be
regarded as the seat of hysteria. But perhaps because hysteria and
hypochondria could not be identified with consistent characteristics,
they eventually come to be understood in terms of an ethic of nervous
sensibility. It is only at this point that the two diseases definitively
join the world of madness. Hysteria and hypochondria are said to
be caused by irritation of the nervous system resulting from over-
stimulation. Thus all of the objects of desire are possible causes of
nervous disorders, but only if the desire for them was overindulged.
Treating hysteria and hypochondria as diseases of moral sensibility
paves the way for nineteenth-century psychology, since the patient's
behavior is in part responsible and thus the patient is guilty of her
own illness.

Although the houses of confinement did not usually provide any
kind of therapy for the mad, there was a therapeutics of madness
practiced during the classical age by physicians outside the hospital.
The cures that were prescribed were aimed at the entire individual,
his nervous fiber as well as his imagination. Thus physical cures
were derived from moral perception. Foucault lists four therapies,
each of which corresponds to a distinct moral problem. "Consoli-
dation" was therapy for the weakness that madness always entailed;
the fibers were not strong enough to resist the irritations. A cure
was needed to give the spirits of fibers a calm vigor. Iron was often
prescribed because it was both the most solid and the most docile

of elements. "Purification" was called for by all of the images of clogging, fermenting, and corruption of liquids and spirits that characterized madness. The ideal of purification would be the complete exchange of bad blood for good, but that was not possible. Transfusions of calves' blood, for example, were administered on a smaller scale, however. "Immersion" involved both the notion of rebirth familiar from baptism and the notion of impregnation that altered the qualities of liquids or solids. Various kinds of baths were prescribed for all forms of madness, including surprise baths and, especially, cold baths. Water had powers of impregnation and it could carry with it secondary qualities like heat and cold. "Regulation of movement" was prescribed in order to return the body, the ideas, and nervous fibers to controlled mobility. Walking and running were ordered to limber and strengthen the body and distribute the humors and juices. The motion of the sea was regarded as most natural and regular, and hence long sea voyages were prescribed for melancholics. Regulation of movement became in the nineteenth century a form of psychological regulation, as in the Mason Cox rotary machine that spun patients around at great speed, not to affect their spirits or fibers, but to frighten and punish them.

Other therapies proper to the classical age reflect a breakdown of the connection between the physical and the moral. Thus the old treatments are no longer considered completely efficacious, and separate ones are required for body and soul. But these new therapies are not psychological. For example, a music cure seems entirely psychological to us, but classical physicians understood music to work directly on the body by imposing qualities upon it. The stimulation of anger was used to promote the discharge of bile. The difference between physical and psychological treatments becomes clear only when fear is used not to arrest movement but as punishment, and when joy signifies not organic expansion but reward. Three additional therapies tried to work on unreason itself. Awakening sought to force the patient out of her delirium; a gun going off near a young girl cured her of convulsions. Theatrical representation used the patient's delirium against itself. For example, a man who refused to eat because he believed himself to be dead was persuaded to eat by a group of actors dressed as the dead setting up a table and eating a meal in his presence. The return to the immediate sought to cure madness by simply exposing the patient to labor and by denying him all of those pleasures that are artificial, unreal, imaginary. In this therapy, patients were returned to their places in the natural order of beings. But even these last cures are not psychological because they do not treat madness as a moral disease, and they still preserve the unity of body and soul.

The end of the great confinement, which will be formally marked by the mythologized act of Pinel in releasing the mad from their chains at Bicêtre, is preceded by what Foucault labels "the great fear": "Suddenly, in a few years in the middle of the eighteenth century, a fear arose—a fear formulated in medical terms but animated, basically, by a moral myth. People were in dread of a mysterious disease that spread, it was said, from the houses of confinement and would soon threaten the cities" (MC 202). The evil that people had attempted to confine seemed now to be concentrated rather than controlled. The authorities were forced by public outcry in the wake of these rumors to acknowledge poor sanitary conditions of Bicêtre. Thus the reform movements of the latter half of the eighteenth century were not motivated by humanitarian concerns for the prisoners, but by fear of Unreason, now imagined in the guise of terrifying disease, a new leprosy. This return of the repressed was a kind of liberation of images that had (like convicts, paupers, and the mad) been confined, images of the monsters that had once found expression in the paintings of Bosch and Brueghel.

But these images of human desire did not emerge unscathed from the social experience of confinement. Rather, in the work of the Marquis de Sade, confinement itself becomes paradoxically an image of desire. Foucault argues that Sadism is not as old as Eros itself, but is "a massive cultural fact which appeared precisely at the end of the eighteenth century, and which constitutes one of the greatest conversions of Western imagination: unreason transformed into delirium of the heart, madness of desire, the insane dialogue of love and death in the limitless presumption of appetite" (MC 210). Unreason is no longer the image of the world as it was to Renaissance painters envisioning the apocalypse, but appears as language and desire. New causes for madness are perceived which are attributed to specific historical or social conditions. Thus too much liberty, as was believed to exist in England, could cause madness, and so could religious anxiety or too much civilization. Novels, for example, could cause madness because they were artificial and detached the soul from the immediate.

The result of this new appearance of unreason in the midst of the

Age of Reason was a new recognition of the difference of the mad from others under confinement. In the late eighteenth century, poverty came to be recognized as a matter of economics and not morality, and the poor were perceived to be more valuable as a reserve labor force. It began to be demanded that the mad and the criminals in houses of confinement be kept separate since the prisoners deserved better than being lumped in with the insane. "The presence of the mad appears as an injustice; but *for others*" (MC 228, italics in original). The necessity of the confinement of unreason, of confinement as a general practice, was no longer evident, but this was also not motivated by humanitarian concern. One regulation of the period classified the mad with vicious and dangerous animals, rather than with criminals. Of human threats, only dangerous criminals and the mad were to be confined, but where the latter were to be kept was unclear since there were no hospitals designed for them.

The stage is thus set for the birth of the asylum. In many respects, *Madness and Civilization* seems designed principally as a reinterpretation of this event. The event itself is not the actual founding of an institution, but the change in practice that has historically been credited to Tuke and Pinel. It was Pinel who went to Bicêtre and proclaimed that "I am convinced that these madmen are so intractable only because they have been deprived of air and liberty" (*MC* 242). Around the same time in England, the Society of Friends established the Retreat, an institution for the insane, under the direction of William Tuke. It is described not as a prison but as a large farm, a house surrounded by a large walled garden. What Tuke and Pinel have in common according to Foucault is that both used a new kind of fear and a new kind of guilt. The mad are no longer made to feel guilty for being mad, but instead must be made to feel morally responsible for anything they may do to disturb society: "Tuke created an asylum where he substituted for the free terror of madness the stifling anguish of responsibility; fear no longer reigned on the other side of the prison gates, it now raged under the seals of conscience. . . . The asylum no longer punished the madman's guilt, it is true; but it did more, it organized that guilt" (*MC* 247). A regime of work and observation was established. Work imposed moral order on the patient, while observation allowed the keepers to discover any concealed signs of madness. Such observation involved formal social gatherings such as tea parties to which several patients were invited and were asked to "dress in their best clothes and vie with each other in politeness and propriety" (MC 249). Members of the staff would then observe the "guests" for any signs of disorder or awkwardness. Tuke's vision was to create a religious community that took the family as its model and that treated the patients as children.

Pinel also wanted his patients to learn bourgeois moral values, but he insisted that religious images be banned from the asylum because religion was regarded as one cause of madness. But the moral content of religion, filtered of its passions and threats, could restore the mad to what is immediate and most essential: moral truth. Yet Pinel's conception of the immediate did not involve putting the patient in a space of nature. Rather, regimentation and legislation provided a site for the inculcation of morality to take place. Several means were used to bring this inculcation about. Silence might be used to force a patient to abandon his delirium. Thus Pinel freed from the irons a patient who believed he was Christ. It was ordered that he was not to be spoken to by anyone in the institution. This caused him to feel humiliated and finally he gave up his delusions and joined the other patients. But Foucault notes that deliverance here is paradoxical. For the madman, the dungeon and the chains had been "the very element of his liberty. . . . Delivered from his chains, he is now chained, by silence, to transgression and to shame. . . . His torment was his glory; his deliverance must humiliate him" (MC 261). In addition to silence, Pinel added "recognition by mirror" and "perpetual judgment" as techniques that forced the patient to internalize morality by making him observe himself and by providing swift punishment for offenses he commits.

Both Pinel and Tuke bring to the asylum a new kind of authority, the authority of the medical personage. These men did not introduce science into the treatment of the mad, but did rely on the authority of science to establish a personality that mastered, rather than knew, the patient's insanity. Psychiatric practice that begins here with Tuke and Pinel is for Foucault a moral tactic that depends on the doctor—patient couple for its effects. Freud, at the end of the nineteenth century, will be the first to actually understand this principle and investigate it rather than cover it up.

This reinterpretation of the birth of the asylum is designed to call into question psychiatry's own history of itself. But Foucault never deals with the history of psychiatry proper since it does not begin until the nineteenth century. But his rereading of what might be called the prehistory of psychiatry would profoundly change our way of thinking about the discipline itself. Mark Cousins and Athar Hussain, who have called Foucault's work a "counter-history of psychiatry" offer psychiatry's version of its own prehistory: "at first doctors intervened in the asylum in their non-medical capacity to sweep aside the barbarous practices and create a humane environment needed for cure. Once the ground was laid, they cast aside their non-medical personae, donned their professional caps and set to analyzing and curing madness, thereby creating psychiatry."[1] But Foucault argues that, on the contrary, psychiatry cannot be identified merely with its analyses and cures, nor can its positivistic understanding of these be accepted. Psychiatry is made possible by the concatenation of institutional internment—continued rather than abolished by Tuke and Pinel—and the separation of the mental from the physical on moral grounds. Prior to Tuke and Pinel, madness was perceived as one kind of unreason and as a disease of both body and soul; though the mad were guilty of their unreason, they were guilty in the manner that lepers were guilty of leprosy: they were not responsible for curing themselves. After Tuke and Pinel, the mad were perceived to have failed, rather than to be afflicted. Their responsibility for that failure was the condition of the possibility of a cure. But in treating their own madness as failure, they made it, made themselves objects of their own judgment. Madness was once again silenced, this time as immorality. Thus "the asylum of the age of positivism, which it is Pinel's glory to have founded, is not the free realm of observation, diagnosis, and therapeutics; it is a juridical space where one is accused, judged, and condemned, and from which one is never released except by the version of this trial in psychological depth—that is, by remorse" (*MC* 269).

    Madness now and always. Foucault concludes *Madness and Civilization* by returning to the focus on art with which he began the book. In the preface he had described his task as an "archaeology" of the silence to which madness has been condemned by the language of psychiatry (*MC* xi). The Middle Ages and the Renaissance allowed madness a voice, but the classical age silenced madness and prepared the way for psychiatry. The conclusion deals with those peeps or screams that escape the padded cell to which madness is confined.

What we hear of madness since Tuke and Pinel we hear in art. Goya, whose work is contemporary with that of Tuke and Pinel, painted madness in confinement. But in his etchings and in his Black Paintings he also depicted the madness "of man cast into darkness" (*MC* 280). This is not the madness of Bosch and Brueghel, for it does not foretell of the next world, but in fact tells of no world at all. For Foucault, Goya gives us forms that arise out of nothing, out of the nothing which is the unreason of the classical age. This is a madness entirely foreign to its contemporaries, but which is nonetheless expressed in Goya and in de Sade and perceived by Nietzsche and Artaud who in turn give madness a new form of speech. "After Sade and Goya, and since them, unreason has belonged to whatever is decisive, for the modern world, in any work of art: that is, whatever any work of art contains that is both murderous and constraining" (*MC* 285). Madness is silenced by psychiatry, but it is expressed now, not so much in the work as in the lives of artists. Thus madness and work are locked in mortal combat.

The philosophy of Nietzsche, the poetry of Hölderlin, the painting of Van Gogh reflect their madness, but the work is not itself mad, is not the product of madness. *"Where there is a work of art, there is no madness;* and yet madness is contemporary with the work of art. . . . The moment when, together, the work of art and madness are born and fulfilled is the beginning of the time when the world finds itself arraigned by that work of art and responsible before it for what it is" (*MC* 288–289, italics in original). Thus in art, Foucault argues, madness finds a way to judge the world, rather than providing the world with a way to know madness. The modern world has been unable to use its language of reason to justify itself in the face of this judgment.

One of the major criticisms of *Madness and Civilization* has focused on this conclusion as an example of Foucault's treatment of madness as a kind of transcendental truth in spite of his explicit desire not to do so. It is generally agreed that Foucault avoids one of the ways in which he might commit this error. He does not treat madness in terms of modern classifications of mental illness. Earlier discussions of madness are not seen as part of some continued progress toward the truth of today's psychiatry. This, as I argued earlier, is one of the theoretical departures that this book makes. What Foucault is accused of, however, is treating the various historical languages about madness as if they all concealed a timeless truth that is revealed in bits and pieces in the works of artists and other visionaries. Thus Dreyfus and Rabinow argue that "It is only a slight distortion of the text to substitute 'madness' for 'the Word of God' and apply Foucault's own criticism of hermeneutics, which he calls exegesis, to his suggestion that madness is a deep secret experience, masked by rationality and discourse, of what it is to be human."[2] Foucault's position is that there are no such experiences, no essence of humanity that the interpretation of human products could reveal, yet madness seems to be precisely such an essential category in *Madness and Civilization*. The problem is not just in the treatment of works of art, but in the very project of trying to deal with madness itself, rather than with psychiatry. Jacques Derrida has argued the impossibility of speaking of madness itself because one is forced to use language and logic that are of reason and not of madness.[3] Derrida's criticism might be extended to most of Foucault's work because it frequently depends upon its claim to suspend contemporary discourse and give us an untainted picture of the historical discourse under discussion. Dreyfus and Rabinow, on the other hand, see Foucault's lapse into hermeneutics in *Madness and Civilization* as something he is able to avoid in *The Birth of the Clinic* and after.

A second criticism of *Madness and Civilization* is not theoretical, but a reaction to what has been perceived as the book's practical impact on the treatment of the insane. In his essay "Foucault and the Bag Lady," a physician named Gerald Weismann attacks Foucault for having been partly responsible for the policy of deinstitutionalization that has put many formerly confined patients out on the streets. The theory is that patients "will be more humanely treated, or achieve greater personal integration, if they are permitted to freely mix with the 'community.' "[4] Foucault is alleged to hold a nostalgia for a golden age of madness, the Middle Ages, when the mad were "integrated," and to seek to bring this situation about today. Weismann reads Foucault as attacking Pinel for failing to liberate the mad and therefore as opposing the asylum and psychiatry as a whole. This is a misreading of Foucault's attitude toward Tuke and Pinel. In spite of his sometimes ironic tone, he does not question their motives; in his view of history, individual motives explain little. *Madness and Civilization* argues that most of the changes that led to the asylum were not motivated by concern for the mad. Since these changes were in fact quite disparate, Foucault would "jettison 'humanitarianism' altogether as a category of analysis."[5]

Although Foucault has frequently been attacked by psychiatrists, his connection to the deinstitutionalization movement is extremely tenuous. It is true that radical psychologist R. D. Laing published the English translation, *Madness and Civilization*, in his series on existentialism and phenomenology, and that Laing later became the most prominent spokesperson for the antipsychiatry movement. Foucault himself regarded the antipsychiatry movement as a radical challenge to the power of the doctor and of reason over madness.[6] Sheridan suggests that Laing was influenced by Foucault to move from Sartrean existential psychology to the more radical opposition to contemporary psychiatric practice with which Laing has since become identified.[7] Foucault himself, however, has nothing directly to say about contemporary psychiatry in *Madness and Civilization*. Furthermore, although deinstitutionalization is consistent with antipsychiatry, they are not identical, since the former depends on the theory that drugs can sufficiently normalize the mad to allow them to function in society, while the latter is also a critique of society. Most importantly, however, Foucault is not a reformer. As John Rajchman puts it, Foucault "parts company with Laing or Szasz; he advanced no alternative theory about the nature and treatment of mental disease."[8] His books rigorously refrain from proposing solutions to the problems they identify, and even his work with the prison group, GIP, involved only the demand that prisoners' voices be heard, and not that specific reforms in prison conditions be made. Foucault would surely not regard the condition of homelessness as preferable to confinement, but rather would see it as yet another form of exclusion to which the mad are subjected.

The relation of *Madness and Civilization* to Foucault's later work has been debated by many of his commentators and explicators. Sheridan argues that the greatest rupture in Foucault's work—but also between it and its cultural period—occurs with this book, which Sheridan says "constitutes the first, essential stage in a radically new analysis of Western civilization since the Renaissance."[9] Dreyfus and Rabinow, on the other hand, play down the significance of this book by treating it as an expression of the hermeneutics that Foucault will get beyond in later work. Both points of view have some merit. The general outline of a historical analysis that will inform all of Foucault's work through *Discipline and Punish* first occurs in *Madness and Civilization*. As Barthes observed, Foucault treats madness not as an object of knowledge but as nothing other than knowledge itself, and this is an approach to the past and to knowledge that Foucault will never abandon.[10] Yet Foucault himself felt that the book was too much a history of modes of perception of an extra-discursive referent (*AK* 47). And although he later stated that he believed that both *Madness and Civilization* and *The Birth of the Clinic* were really about power, this theme is not explicit in either of them. Thus, we might understand *Madness and Civilization* as a work that makes a major methodological breakthrough in its historical treatment of madness, but that remains in other respects tied to an older intellectual history Foucault will later come to reject.

The Clinic and the Gaze

If the importance of *Madness and Civilization* in Foucault's oeuvre is sometimes questioned, that of *The Birth of the Clinic: An Archaeology of Medical Perception* often seems to be very slight indeed. Sheridan describes it as a mere "extended postscript" to *Madness and Civilization* and Karlis Racevskis calls it "not as successful as other works."[11] In many respects this book differs significantly from Foucault's other studies, even from the ones that also deal with the histories of institutions. One of the powerful attractions of Foucault's work has been its historical sweep. *Madness and Civilization*, *The Order of Things*, and *Discipline and Punish* all deal with the entirety of what historians call the modern period, everything that follows the Middle Ages. *The Birth of the Clinic*, on the other hand, deals nominally with the years 1720–1820, and actually concentrates on an even shorter period of time at the end of the eighteenth century when most of the innovations in medical practice it discusses came into being. While madness or man himself—who is said in *The Order of Things* to be about to disappear—are likely to be of interest to humanistically minded intellectuals, medical perception is arcane enough to put off even socially or scientifically oriented readers. Furthermore, *The Birth of the Clinic* relies even more heavily than did *Madness and Civilization* on what has come to be called "the archive," the reading of historical records and contemporary documents that have been abandoned by the traditional or official histories. In using the archive, one reads everything from a particular period relevant to one's subject. The earlier work had been based in part on the archive, but it had also made use of major cultural works such as those of Bosch and Shakespeare. *The Birth of the Clinic,* however, restricts itself to the recovery of ancient medical documents and treatises from which it liberally quotes and which are at times rigorously analyzed. Although Foucault will continue to make use of the archive in later works, *The Birth of the Clinic* is certainly the most restricted in using it. Because *The Birth of the Clinic* deals with a smaller subject and makes smaller claims than do Foucault's other major works, it may deserve some of its relative neglect. Nevertheless, the book does advance the general approach of *Madness and Civilization* in several important ways, and it introduces the "gaze," a concept that, although it does not reappear under that name in Foucault's later work, is itself a major innovation in the development of Foucault's ideas about power, knowledge, and the subject.

The Birth of the Clinic begins with images that are even more startling than those of *Madness and Civilization.* These images serve the same function as the ones in the earlier work—to throw the reader off guard, but they also serve a new one: to present a vivid comparison of what doctors saw before and after the development of clinical medicine.

Towards the middle of the eighteenth century, Pomme treated and cured a hysteric by making her take "baths, ten or twelve hours a day, for ten whole months." At the end of this treatment for the desiccation of the nervous system and the heat that sustained it, Pomme saw "membranous tissues like pieces of damp parchment . . . peel away with some slight discomfort, and these were passed daily with the urine; the right ureter also peeled away and came out whole in the same way." The same thing occurred with the intestines, which at another stage, "peeled off their internal tunics, which we saw emerge from the rectum. The esophagus, the arterial trachea, and the tongue also peeled in due course; and the patient had rejected different pieces either by vomiting or by expectoration."

Less than a hundred years later, this is how a doctor observed an anatomical lesion of the brain and its enveloping membranes, the so-called "false membranes" frequently found on patients suffering from "chronic meningitis": "Their outer surface, which is next to the arachnoidian layer of the dura matter, adheres to this layer, sometimes very lightly, when they can be separated easily, sometimes very firmly and tightly, in which case it can be very difficult to detach them. . . . The organization of the false membranes also displays a great many differences: the thin ones are buffy, like the albuminous skins of eggs, and have no distinctive structure of their own. Others, on one of their sides, often display traces of blood vessels crossing over one another in different directions and injected. (*BC* ix–x)

Foucault's emphasis in these examples is on what each physician saw, and he notes that the differences are both tiny and total. Pierre Pomme sees what to us is fantasy. Gaspard-Laurent Bayle sees the encephalic lesions of general paralysis in a way that would be recognizable to contemporary doctors. We are sure that Pomme could not have seen what he claims he saw, but how is our certainty possible? And how was it that Pomme could believe what he did, and yet less than one hundred years later, the terrain of medicine could be so totally different? For Foucault, the answer involves seeing only in so far as it is conditioned by discourse. But seeing is in Foucault's view nearly wholly conditioned by discourse. That is why Foucault rejects the explanation that the change in medical perception from Pomme to Bayle is brought about by simple empiricism, a return to what is seen from the distortions of belief ungrounded in the visible. Rather, to understand this change, this mutation in discourse, we need to examine the region where words and things, seeing and saying, are still one. It is this same region that Foucault will explore much more widely in *The Order of Things,* the French title of which translates as "Words and Things." In *The Birth of the Clinic,* however, Foucault will focus on the narrow field of medical seeing and saying. What he will find is that although discourse determines what is seen, the act of looking, or the gaze, will define the patient's relationship to the doctor and to medical knowledge.

The basic argument of *The Birth of the Clinic* is that in the late eighteenth century a new form of medicine came into being which Foucault calls "anatomo-clinical" because it is dependent upon two new forms of medical practice that begin at this time: the clinic as a site of diagnosis and teaching, and pathological anatomy as the foundation of medical knowledge. Earlier medicine had focused its attention on classifying diseases according to their essences which were described in various treatises of nosography. In this sort of medicine, the actual body of the patient was obscured by the search for the essential disease so that treatment might be delayed until the disease could be truly classified, the patient's body actually being regarded as an impediment to knowing the disease itself. Traditionally, the shift away from this medicine of essences is attributed to a return to pure, unbiased examination of the patient, a "return" because medicine writes its own history so as to portray the clinical relationship as the historical condition on which medicine has always rested. The freedom of the gaze in the restored clinic is traditionally credited with the changes in medicine that occur in the late eighteenth century. But Foucault argues that the clinic is both older and younger than the traditional narrative suggests. It is younger because the earliest clinics were established in the seventeenth century; they cannot be traced back to Hippocrates. But clinics are older in that they are not new in the eighteenth century, and neither are such practices as keeping records of individual cases or examining the patient. The change that occurs in the late eighteenth century is not the appearance of the clinic, or the invention of pathological anatomy, but the creation of a new form of medicine out of the combination of the two. This combination is in turn made possible by the application of grammatical and probabilistic structures that "freed medical perception from the play of essence and symptoms, and from the no less ambiguous play of species and individuals" (*BC* 105). The medicine that deciphered symptoms as the sacred text of an invisible disease disappears and is replaced by a medicine of lesions that were the disease, of organs that were its site: "it is no longer a pathological species inserting itself into the body wherever possible; it is the body itself that has become ill" (*BC* 136). Thus the new method was not the result of a long and continuous historical development, but of "a recasting at the level of epistemic knowledge (*savoir*) itself" (*BC* 137). In other words, what changed was not the practice of examining the patient, but what it was possible for the doctor to see during the examination.

Foucault tells us at the beginning of *The Birth of the Clinic* that it is a book "about space, about language, and about death; it is about the act of seeing, the gaze" (*BC* ix). At the end of the book he tells us that it is "an attempt to apply a method in the confused, under-structured, and ill-structured domain of the history of ideas" (*BC* 195). The method Foucault applies is more or less structuralism. The first French edition of *The Birth of the Clinic* was more explicitly structuralist than the second edition, from which the English version is translated, where Foucault changed the term "language" to "discourse" and changed many instances of use of the terms "signifier" and "signified." Foucault later denied being a structuralist, saying in *The Order of Things* that he used "none of the methods, concepts, or key terms that characterize structural analysis" (*OT* xiv). Nonetheless, the evidence of structuralism's influence is readily apparent throughout *The Birth of the Clinic,* which he labels a "structural study" (*BC* xix). Why does it matter whether Foucault is a structuralist or not? Because if we were to treat him as a thoroughgoing structuralist, it would seriously distort one of the principal assumptions and distinguishing features of his work. As Dreyfus and Rabinow point out, Foucault never sought atemporal structures, but rather historically changing conditions of possibility.[12] But adherents of structuralism—as typified by French anthropologist Claude Lévi-Strauss, who hypothesized a "savage mind" shared by all humans and characterized by a group of relationships between the essential terms of experience—do seek such natural, nonhistorical structures. Structuralism derives from linguist Ferdinand de Saussure who described language as a system of purely differential relations among phonemes, the elementary sounds that make up a speech. Saussure also distinguished the basic semantic or meaning element of language as the relationship between signifier and signified, the sound or print on the one hand, and the idea meant by the signifier on the other. Saussure's emphasis on relational structures gave structuralism its name. Lévi-Strauss found that such an approach could explain much about human cultures, while semioticians such as Roman Jacobson and A. J. Greimas extrapolated from natural language to all communication. Where Foucault differs from Lévi-Strauss is that he does not believe these structures are essential to human nature. Rather, his whole project is to show how structures change radically at certain moments in history.

What Foucault borrows from structuralism is its assumption that oppositions between a few key terms "structure," provide the conditions of possibility for, thought or discourse in a given time, place, and discussion. This borrowing is significant because it distinguishes *The Birth of the Clinic* from *Madness and Civilization.* The earlier work treated madness as a historically changing concept, the meaning of which was determined by the differing ideas and practices of the Middle Ages, the Renaissance, the classical age, etc. Furthermore, madness itself seems to be there lurking behind all of these shifting meanings without ever being capable of finding expression in the languages of reason that are its very antithesis.

This analysis differed from the usual methods of the history of science because it steadfastly refused to read the categories of modern psychiatry back into earlier periods. But *Madness and Civilization* continued to share with traditional history of ideas an interest in the self-understanding of historical actors. Thus the changing meaning of madness is not a product of some deep structural transformation. In *The Birth of the Clinic*, however, what doctors such as Pinel and Bichat actually thought they were doing is irrelevant; what Foucault looks at are structures that govern the gaze from below without the historical participants being aware of them. This general form of analysis will be important in both *The Order of Things* and in *The Archaeology of Knowledge*.

The influence of structuralism also helps to explain some seemingly mysterious language in *The Birth of the Clinic*. What are we to make, for example, of Foucault asserting that the book is about space, language, death, and the gaze? We will discover that three of the terms—space, language, and the gaze—are explained soon enough, but death must wait until chapter 8, more than halfway through the book. The basic contention is that it is pathological anatomy which makes possible the development of the clinical medicine whose birth Foucault is chronicling. This may seem at first glance like a mere technical innovation, but Foucault says that in the late eighteenth century it was neither an innovation—the dissection of corpses had been an accepted medical practice since the Renaissance—nor merely technical. Rather, the dissection of corpses leads to a change in the conception of the relationship between life and death. Thus we get sentences such as the following: "Life, disease, and death now form a technical and conceptual trinity. The continuity of the age-old beliefs that placed the threat of disease in life and of the approaching presence of death in disease is broken; in its place is articulated a triangular figure the summit of which is defined by death" (*BC* 144). Here Foucault describes death as the vantage point of the medical gaze, the point from which life and disease can be seen. Prior to this, both life and death had made disease invisible, it being literally concealed by the living body and obscured by the effects of death. That is the technical triangle that the birth of clinical medicine rolls over.

The conceptual triangle treats each term as part of a deep structure of discourse, like the triangle of the raw, the cooked, and the rotten (Figure 1) that Lévi-Strauss uses to discuss the structure of culinary

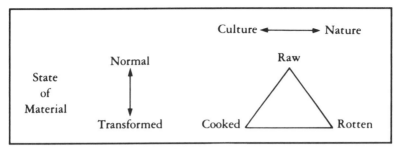

Figure 1. The Culinary Triangle

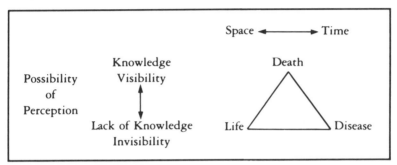

Figure 2. The Triangle of Medical Perception

customs and beliefs.[13] The significance of the terms is revealed by their position relative to two scales, a vertical one that runs from normal to transformed and a horizontal one that opposes culture and nature. Thus cooking is cultural while rotting is natural, but raw, domesticated food could be considered both cultural and natural. Raw food is untransformed, but both cooking and rotting are transformations.

In Figure 2, Foucault's vertical scale would put knowledge or visibility at the top and lack of knowledge or invisibility at the bottom. The horizontal scale is an opposition of space and time. Foucault explains the change in medical perception by calling for a shift in the position of the three terms so that death is now seen as yielding knowledge and as mediating between the space of the organism and the time of disease. There are some further permutations of these relationships: "And beneath the chronological life/disease/death relation, another, earlier, deeper figure is traced: that which links life and death, and so frees, besides, the signs of disease"

(*BC* 155). Lévi-Strauss's model shows the kind of thinking Foucault is engaged in here, and may help one to visualize what Foucault has in mind when he speaks of finding the "deep structures" of the visible (*BC* 90). In *The Order of Things* we see Foucault make use of another structuralist conception of the relations between key terms, that one represented by a rectangle or quadrilateral (see chapter 4).

If the use of structuralist techniques is the central methodological innovation of *The Birth of the Clinic*, the gaze is its most influential concept. The English word *gaze* is a relatively unusual choice to translate the French *regard*, a common word normally translated as "look." "Gaze" is used because "look" has the additional connotation in English of referring to the thing being observed, so that if the French *le regard médical* were translated "the medical look" it would sound like a style of clothing. As Martin Jay has pointed out, however, in Foucault's discussion of *le regard* it is hard not to hear echoes of Jean-Paul Sartre's well-known account of "the look" (as *le regard* is translated there) in *Being and Nothingness*.[14] Sartre argued that to be caught by the look of another is to be objectified and rendered a thing rather than a subject or person, and as a result to feel shamed, alienated, enslaved, and even endangered by the other.[15] Sartre's discussion has given *le regard* negative connations that are not blunted by Foucault's use of the term to discuss the domination of the visual. Jay argues that Foucault's oeuvre is part of a movement of "anti-ocular" thought in twentieth-century France that has attacked the primacy that sight has held in Western culture.[16] This primacy is easily illustrated by the number of visual metaphors that are regularly used to discuss thoughts or ideas: perspective, point of view, to see another's point, etc. In addition, many terms, such as "theory," that are no longer literal references to sight are etymologically related to it. "To see something" means metaphorically to perceive it as it is without the bias or distortions of mere thought. But it is Foucault's point that we never "see" things in this way. The gaze is a matter of applying a language or a mathematics to the thing seen so that it is constituted by the observer in his terms. Thus the gaze suggests that knowledge forms at the intersection of seeing and speaking.

The problematic of the individual as both subject and object is one that Foucault will take up explicitly in *The Order of Things* and that will remain a focus of attention throughout the rest of his career. He will deal with it specifically in terms of the visual in *Discipline and Punish,* where the notion of the gaze as visual domination is extended in the concept of panoptic surveillance. Here, the implications of the power of the gaze over its object are clear. In *The Birth of the Clinic,* the issue of power remains in the background. There is little discussion of the doctor–patient relationship that figured prominently in *Madness and Civilization,* so we are not likely to understand the gaze as an imposition on the patient. But in the context of the two other books it is hard not to see it that way. When he wrote *The Birth of the Clinic,* Foucault seems to have been more interested in attacking the myth of empiricism than in observing the effects of power. However, the concept of the gaze is a contribution to that latter project because it shows how even the apparently simple act of seeing is always conditioned by the discourse and practices in which it takes place. Thus it will provide the grounds for Foucault's later insight that to be examined is to be subjected to the examiner and to the norm.

Madness and Civilization and *The Birth of the Clinic* both derive their power from the reversal of earlier narratives that had come to be accepted as the truth about the origins of modern psychiatry and modern medicine. Although Foucault performs his reversal on grounds specific to each field, in one sense it is the same narrative that Foucault has rewritten. That narrative is one of scientific and humanitarian progress. These two virtues are related in that science is supposed to make greater humanitarianism possible, while humanitarianism, like science, is supposed to be objective, a response grounded in the essence of what it is to be human, what Foucault will later attack as humanism. What Foucault shows in both books is that progress is never unambiguous; psychiatry develops out of physical confinement and mental punishment, medicine must take a detour through death in the form of pathological anatomy. He also shows that what seems to occur for humanitarian motives, or from the motive of the pure quest for truth, usually has other, more persuasive explanations in the power of discourse to shape the practice of individuals and societies. To do this is not only to tell stories about the origins of the asylum and the clinic, but also to find a new way to tell stories about intellectual events. Foucault refuses to take the history of ideas as a satisfactory way of explaining these events, and substitutes instead a history of practices, discourses, and structures. Thus Foucault challenges in these books some of the most powerful stories we tell about ourselves and our Western civilization.

Chapter Four
The *Episteme* and the Disappearance of Man

Although both *Madness and Civilization* and *The Birth of the Clinic* develop methods and approaches that it will use, there is little in either book that could have led readers to expect *The Order of Things*. While those books dealt with subjects that might both be classified under the category of the history of medical practice, this one covers all of the human sciences from their prehistory in the Renaissance and classical age to their rise and predicted fall in the modern period. Thus *The Order of Things* is as vast and broad as *The Birth of the Clinic* is restricted and narrow. Where the claims of the earlier two books were likely to disturb mainly professionals in psychiatry and historians of medicine, *The Order of Things* has something to offend intellectuals in all disciplines and of all ideologies. The two most shocking items were undoubtedly the division of modern history into three radically discontinuous periods defined by their differing *epistemes*, and the announcement of the disappearance of man with which the book concludes. These were perhaps most offensive to Marxists and other intellectuals on the Left who saw Foucault's history as devoid of both class conflict and revolutionary hope, and his prognosis of man's erasure as a challenge to the values upon which left-wing politics are based. But one should not get the impression that *The Order of Things* was merely notorious, that it lacked a strong favorable reception. On the contrary, *The Order of Things* received largely favorable reviews and its rapid sales are something of a legend in contemporary French intellectual life. Those who were attracted to the book tended to like it for exactly the same breathtaking reversals that others found dismaying.

The subtitle of *The Order of Things* is *An Archaeology of the Human Sciences*. This deserves some discussion since it explains Foucault's goals in writing the book, but may also confuse the reader. The notion of archaeology has received some discussion earlier, and I will take it up again in the next chapter. Here our task is to conceive of this word as an extended metaphor for Foucault's project in *The Order of Things*. First, one does an archaeology most literally of a piece of ground, a space, a region. The region that Foucault is investigating is that of the human sciences, which is itself subdivided into the regions of psychology, sociology, and cultural studies. These regions are not disciplines, but areas of knowledge constituted during the modern period that disciplines may subdivide. Foucault's archaeology of this space, however, ignores its current features, just as an archaeologist ignores the surface level of her site. Foucault's task is not to analyze the human sciences, but to place them in a vertical sequence and to discover their horizontal relations. Thus if we imagine the history of Western knowledge since the Middle Ages as the site of an archaeological dig, we have a general picture of *The Order of Things*. Each *episteme* is like a stratum of earth in which the artifacts uncovered are the products of a distinct historical period. We know this not just by their proximity, but also by their character, which shows their relationship to each other and to the whole. But just as the different strata of earth at a dig site tell us little about why one civilization vanished and another began, so the analysis of *epistemes* tells us nothing about the change from one to another. The archaeologist merely observes that the change has occurred at a certain historical moment.

Nevertheless, an archaeologist will find objects that resemble each other from stratum to stratum. His excavations would be meaningless if this were not the case since he could not recognize, classify, and compare what was uncovered. Thus Foucault finds that knowledge since the Middle Ages has always dealt in one way or another with living beings, with objects of need, and with words. In discussing each *episteme*, Foucault seeks to show the conditions that allowed the particular ways of dealing with these entities to come about. Thus, although *The Order of Things* has a chronological order, it is not a narrative of how we got from the Renaissance to the classical age, and from there to the modern era, but a description of each of these levels by comparison with the others. The modern level is itself subdivided into several more strata, with the human sciences nearly at the top. What Foucault shows in his analysis of this level is how the human sciences are related to forms of knowledge that characterize the period. The human sciences themselves are directly discussed only in the last chapter. Foucault's goal is, then, not to explain where the human sciences came from, but to locate them as mere artifacts of a particular historical formation. To accomplish this goal, Foucault sees himself as having to root out and destroy the assumption that the human sciences deal with questions that are essential to human knowledge throughout history. This in turn requires that we discard all of our other habits of thinking about the history of knowledge, something that *The Order of Things* works at in the multitude of ways.

Two Beginnings

Like *Madness and Civilization*, *The Order of Things* also has two opening gambits that are as different from each other as they are striking. The first beginning is a preface that ascribes the origin of the book to a passage from the Argentinian writer Jorge Luis Borges, and "the laughter that shattered, as I read the passage, all the familiar landmarks of . . . *our* thought." Borge's passage is itself a quotation of a " 'certain Chinese encyclopedia' in which it is written that 'animals are divided into: (a) belonging to the Emperor, (b) embalmed, (c) tame, (d) sucking pigs, (e) sirens, (f) fabulous, (g) stray dogs, (h) included in the present classification, (i) frenzied, (j) innumerable, (k) drawn with a very fine camelhair brush, (l) *et cetera,* (m) having just broken the water pitcher, (n) that from a long way off look like flies.' " What we learn from this taxonomy, says Foucault, is the limitation of our own system of thought, for we immediately understand "the stark impossibility of thinking *that*" (*OT* xv, italics in original).

Like the quotation from Pomme that begins *The Birth of the Clinic,* the Borges taxonomy is both disorienting and illustrative. It is unlike the Pomme passage in the kind of reaction it is likely to provoke, however. In the earlier example, we were convinced that Pomme could not have seen what he claims to have seen, or that his observation was quite simply wrong. But the Borges taxonomy does not offer us even that satisfaction, since taxonomies are neither true nor false. Hence the passage from Borges is more disorienting for it can call into question our usual passive reliance on our own system of order. Foucault's point is that if it is impossible to think this order of things because it differs so radically from our own, then it is also true that our own ordering could easily seem just as impossible to someone who was used to a different order. Foucault's task was relatively easy in contrasting Pomme and Bayle: he wanted to illustrate a massive change in the medical gaze and in medical discourse, a change that occurred within a discrete field of knowledge and was recognized by everyone. In *The Order of Things*, Foucault uses the Borges taxonomy to illustrate the existence of a level or region of knowledge that was unknown to most readers and that coincided with no traditional field or discipline but pertained to all of the disciplines in the quite general category of the human sciences.

As the literal translation of the French title of *The Order of Things*, *Les mots et les choses*, "words and things," suggests, Foucault had identified this region in *The Birth of the Clinic* where he says that to determine the moment of the mutation of medical discourse we must look to the region where words and things have not been separated (*BC* xi). It is this region which Foucault will open up for exploration and mapping in *The Order of Things*. In this work he locates the region between, on the one hand, "empirical orders" established by "the fundamental codes of a culture" governing language, techniques, values, etc., and, on the other hand, scientific theories and philosophical interpretations that explain and justify order (*OT* xx). In discovering this middle region we may realize that our empirical orders are not the only possible ones, but also realize the fact "that order *exists*" (*OT* xx, italics in original). *The Order of Things* is thus an attempt to analyze "the pure experience of order and . . . its modes of being" (*OT* xxi). But Foucault does not mean that order is itself a metaphysical or essential category established outside of the particular conditions of its existence in a given culture. Rather, he is arguing that the general shape of order in a given culture is more fundamental than either its empirical ordering or its theoretical reflections upon order.

To illustrate the three regions, I will consider the questions that might arise from each of them regarding Borges's taxonomy. Questions coming from the first region would ask whether this or that category, "stray dogs" or "frenzied," really belongs there, but it would not question the overall assumptions that govern the system. Questions coming from the region of science and philosophy would ask why this order exists or on what principle it is established. The middle region would produce questions about the order itself: is it continuous or discontinuous? linked to space or to time? In other words, what are the abstract structures or forms that order takes? The analysis of such a region is not history of ideas or science, but a project designed to show how science and theory became possible, to explain the conditions of possibility of knowledge rather than the specific content of the knowledge itself. Foucault's use of Borges's taxonomy helps this region of pure order become visible to the reader, as does the argument of the book as a whole in showing how the fundamental orderings of the Renaissance, the classical age, and the modern period differ from each other nearly as much as the Borges taxonomy does from one found in a zoology textbook.

The very real difficulty and disorientation of the preface may seem slight, however, when compared to that encountered in the next several chapters of *The Order of Things*. Chapter 1, "Las Meninas," is actually not disorienting except in the labyrinthine difficulty of its interpretation of the Velàzquez painting from which it draws its name. This second beginning of *The Order of Things* is meant to illustrate an instance of the kind of order discussed in the preface by focusing on the problem of representation in the classical age. It is also intended, we are entitled to suppose, to illustrate that someone more or less belonging to the period was aware of, or at least gave expression to, the character of its *episteme*. The fact that Foucault has chosen to do this by means of the interpretation of a painting remains surprising even though art played an important role in *Madness and Civilization*. It is surprising because Foucault is no longer doing the kind of intellectual history he was in the earlier volume in which art could be said to express ideas and attitudes. Moreover, while Foucault made considerable use of artistic works in the earlier volume, he did not perform an extended interpretation of any of them. Rather than working out detailed readings, Foucault was content to let the paintings stand for the ideas he was discussing. Nothing could be further from his treatment of *Las Meninas*, which is an extremely close reading that seems to depend on quite technical arguments about perspective and visual projection to support its major claims.

John Rajchman has offered a persuasive explanation of the importance of art in Foucault's oeuvre and of the role of *Las Meninas* in *The Order of Things*. Rajchman argues that Foucault was heavily influenced by modernist literature and theories of literature such as the *nouvelle critique* (French new criticism, not to be confused with Anglo-American New Criticism) of Roland Barthes that were designed to underwrite modernist writing. Such criticism reads art as self-referential so that instead of telling us about reality in general, art and literature are said to refer only to the literary or artistic tradition of which they are a part. Rajchman points out that Foucault reads *Las Meninas, Don Quixote,* and the works of de Sade, such as *Justine,* in just this way.[1] But this self-referentiality is compromised to some extent in *The Order of Things* where art and literature are presented as having privileged access to the *episteme* of their time. Literature and art are not knowledges and thus are not ordered by the *episteme* of their era. An *episteme* is not a worldview or a Zeitgeist, but a configuration that structures thought and knowledge only of a particular group of disciplines. But literature may articulate the limits of this configuration, and thus "is *about* it as a whole. . . . Arts are meta-epistemic, allegories of the deep arrangements that make knowledge possible."[2] Thus it is the modernist privileging of art as the avant garde that explains the importance given to Velàzquez's *Las Meninas* in *The Order of Things.* The painting can reveal the *episteme* of the classical age because it is not subject to that *episteme.* The fact that the *episteme* governs all thought and knowledge within the human sciences makes it impossible for those sciences to know their own current *episteme.* But art lies outside of the *episteme* and therefore is able to reveal the *episteme* of its own time at least to one looking back.

Foucault reads *Las Meninas* as an allegory of classical representation. In many respects the painting seems made for the part it plays in *The Order of Things.* The painting depicts a painter—it is Velàzquez in self-portrait—poised in front of a canvas the back of which forms nearly the entire left edge of the painting. In the background we see two prominently lit rectangles among a variety of darker ones, which are themselves paintings. One of the lighter rectangles is a mirror in which two figures, a man and a woman, are reflected. The other rectangle is an open doorway from which a man is gazing out at us, seemingly prepared either to leave or enter the room via the stairs on which he is standing. In the foreground to the right of the painter is a group of figures—many of whom are also staring out into the space in front of the painting—including a female child, dwarfs, courtiers, maids of honor, and a dog. According to Foucault, tradition identifies the little girl in the center foreground as the Infanta Margarita, and the figures in the mirror as her parents, King Philip IV and his wife, Mariana, who are serving as models for the painter, the mirror telling us of their presence in the space in front of the painting we are looking at.

Why is this single painting worthy of an entire chapter of a book that will be mainly concerned with the sciences of language, life, and labor? Because it is "the manifest essence" of all representation and "the representation . . . of Classical representation" (*OT* 16). *Las Meninas* serves as a perfect synecdoche for the classical *episteme*, as we will see in a moment. But this answer leaves one somewhat dissatisfied, since *The Order of Things* describes three different *epistemes* but only the classical is illustrated in this way. Another reason for the prominence of *Las Meninas* is the prominence of the problem of representation in modernist literature and in contemporary French criticism and theory. Although it is true that such theory has taught us how to read all art as self-referential, explicitly self-referential art has become particularly highly valued. As a painting about the act of painting, *Las Meninas* seems almost contemporary with such explicitly self-referential work as the writing of Mallarmé or Raymond Roussel. Furthermore, it is not just classical representation that is being represented in *Las Meninas,* but positions of subject and object that, as we have seen, are reciprocal aspects of the gaze. *Las Meninas* is not, or not mainly, an artifact of the classical age. It does not carry the same status as Linnaeus's system of naming and classification of natural species, because it tells us not just about classical representation, but about the limits of representation itself. As such, it may not matter whether Foucault's interpretation of the painting can be sustained on the grounds of projection and perspective he offers.[3] The painting serves in any case to illustrate the table of representation, the various spaces in the grid of relationships that are possible when representation occurs, and it may serve this function whatever Velàzquez intended the painting to be about.

Any act of representation involves three potential positions that human beings may occupy. The representer is the one who makes the representation by painting, writing, taking a photograph, etc. In performing such an act, the representer is the subject who knows or sees. The represented is one who is being painted or photographed or written about, and as such is the object of the representation. The representee is one for whom the representation is made. In seeing the representation, the representee is also a subject. Now in *Las Meninas,* each of these positions is in some way displayed, although we will not say each is actually present in the painting. Obviously, the self-portrait of Velàzquez provides the place of the representer. The objects to be represented by the painter, the king and queen, are visible in the mirror. The man on the stairs in the lighted doorway at the rear is described by Foucault as a spectator, one who could a few moments ago have been standing in front of the scene depicted in *Las Meninas*. And yet, none of these positions of representation is adequately represented. The painter, for example, is not painting but looking out at what presumably are his models. If he were painting, we would not be able to see him for he would be hidden by the canvas. The objects represented are not really here either, but only their reflections in the mirror. Finally, the spectator is properly marginal to the scene, on the verge of leaving or perhaps conducting covert surveillance since, in spite of his brightly lit profile, no one is paying any attention to him. But the spectator is more than marginal to a representation, a painting, a novel: he must be outside of it in order to fulfill his function.

Foucault notes that the gaze of the painter, the Infanta, the spectator in the rear, and several of the other figures is fixed on a point directly in front of the painting. In this space, if the bottom edge of the painting were extended, we would see the king and queen. But we do not see them and thus they occupy in the world of the painting the same space the painter of *Las Meninas* and we as spectators also occupy. "These three 'observing' functions come together in a point exterior to the picture: that is, an ideal point in relation to what is represented, but a perfectly real one too, since it is also the starting-point that makes the representation possible" (*OT* 15). The mirror seems to restore what is lacking in every gaze, the gazer. Velàzquez, the anonymous face of a passerby, the king and his wife, each of these figures should be able to see him or herself in the mirror, which Foucault seems to treat almost as if it were an actual piece of reflective glass integrated into the canvas. But only the king and his wife appear there, and only because they are absent from the picture; the painter and the spectator are present in the picture and therefore cannot be represented in the mirror. The two sovereigns are the center of attention of those in the painting and their symbolic sovereignty as monarchs echoes the sovereignty of the triple gaze that emanates from their place. Nevertheless this center must be absent, because in terms of classical representation, the subject does not appear in the table of representation. There is no place for Linnaeus in his grid of species or for the speaker in general grammar. *Las Meninas* is itself a table on which the world of representations is displayed. "What is represented are the functions of representation. What is not represented is a unified and unifying subject who posits these representations and who makes them objects for himself."[4] This subject will emerge in the modern *episteme*. The painting captures every function of representation except the act of representation itself.

The effect of Foucault's discussion of *Las Meninas* is not, however, to clarify classical representation for most readers. That is because the writing in this chapter is designed to illustrate paradox or ambiguity rather than clarity. Thus "the profound invisibility of what one sees is inseparable from the invisibility of the person seeing" (*OT* 16). This kind of writing is in turn explained by my earlier observation about Foucault's modernist conception of the role of art. As art *Las Meninas* is not supposed to present knowledge in terms of the classical *episteme;* it is supposed to represent the limits of the *episteme*. It does this by illustrating the point at which the *episteme* collapses as a result of its own contradictions. But art not only tells us about the limits of an historical scheme, it also tells us about essential limits. Thus *Las Meninas* can be the "manifest essence" of representation because representation has an essence, which can be revealed, not directly but precisely in terms of its limits. We might imagine representation as a very large enclosure that cannot be mapped or diagrammed because it cannot be apprehended except when one occasionally runs into one of the walls. What *Las Meninas* tells us of profound invisibility is not a function of the classical *episteme*, but of the truth about representation that art can reveal. Art appears, then, to continue to play the same role in *The Order of Things* as it did in the conclusion to *Madness and Civilization* where Van Gogh and others were said to reveal what we might now want to call the profound madness of reason. The problem with this position is that it contradicts other assumptions that Foucault appears to hold, especially the assumption that knowledge is always the product of an *episteme*, and, therefore, that we can never know representation or anything else as an essence. It may be this problem which led Foucault to abandon the analysis of works of art after *The Order of Things*.

Resemblance

The chapter that follows *"Las Meninas"* begins the narrative that *The Order of Things* tells of three successive *epistemes* and the changes in knowledge that result from each. Yet even this chapter, "The Prose of the World," could be described as yet another introduction, one that also serves the purpose of disorientation, or as Rajchman puts it, "a defamiliarizing contrast for what follows."[5] If the Borges taxonomy was designed to call into question one's assumptions about order, this chapter is meant to do the same for one's faith in transhistorical knowledge. It is the same point Foucault had tried to make before in his books about madness and medicine: we will misunderstand the past if we read it as an anticipation of what we now believe to be true, or if we assume that it shares what Foucault calls "our positivities," those very ordering structures that define an *episteme,* yet are so much a part of the background of our thought that to call them assumptions would make them seem more accessible than Foucault understands them to be. What makes "The Prose of the World," and much of the rest of *The Order of Things,* doubly disorienting is that Foucault presents his discussion of these ancient positivities as if he were explaining systems of thought he himself shares. He makes no disparaging remarks about these systems, and, more importantly, virtually no comparisons to other *epistemes.* Furthermore, if one is not careful, it is easy to forget where in history and in Foucault's narrative one is, since he makes relatively few references to dates. For example, he begins chapter 2 with several references to the sixteenth and early seventeenth centuries, but he mentions dates only three or four more times in the entire chapter. There is no ambiguity in Foucault's account since everything in the chapter refers to the Renaissance, but given the strangeness of the material and the neutrality of the presentation, some readers may forget this fact.

The first *episteme,* that of the Renaissance, is characterized by resemblance, which "played a constructive role in the knowledge of Western culture. It . . . guided exegesis and the interpretation of texts . . . organized the play of symbols, made possible knowledge of things visible and invisible, and controlled the art of representing them" (*OT* 17). The significance of this claim will doubtless seem greater if we keep in mind that in the classical age—and in structuralist theory—difference is regarded as making language, and therefore knowledge and meaning, possible. While the Renaissance was certainly aware that language performed a kind of representation, language was regarded as the repetition of the thing represented. That it is very hard for us to conceive of a system of knowledge organized around resemblance is something that Foucault is counting on for this chapter to have its disorienting effect. Whether our thinking is the product of literary theory, cultural anthropology, computer science, information theory, or almost any other contemporary intellectual discipline or sphere, we count on difference as a central organizing principle of our knowledge. Consider, for example, the fundamental representational structure of the computer, the binary number system. The computer is able to store and process enormous amounts of information at speeds that defy the imagination by using minute electrical circuits that can represent either "1" or "0" by being open or closed. Such a purely differential relationship is also purely representative since there is no similarity between what the binary number might come to mean within a given application and the number itself.

Even to think about such a similarity strikes us as strange, if not occult. But the Renaissance thought elaborately about similitude, for "if the things that resembled one another were indeed infinite in number" then one needed to "establish the forms according to which they might resemble one another" (*OT* 17). There were four major forms, or figures, of resemblance: 1) *convenientia*, or convenience, describes resemblances between things that are juxtaposed and hence derive properties from one another; *aemulatio*, or emulation, names the way in which things in the universe separated by great distances may reflect one another, as, for example, the human intellect is an imperfect reflection of the mind of God; *analogy* combines both *convenientia* and *aemulatio* to permit resemblances that are neither visible nor essential to the things themselves, but a matter of mere relations; and, finally, *sympathy* perhaps best reveals the Renaissance *episteme*. Because the connections or paths by which it may travel cannot be known in advance, sympathy potentially exists everywhere. But more importantly, sympathy describes not only similitudes that already exist, but also a power that transforms objects to create resemblance. Thus sympathy would turn the world into an undifferentiated glob of sameness if it were not for the compensation of its twin, antipathy, which maintains hatreds between objects so that they do not turn into one another. "Because of the movement and dispersion created by its laws, the sovereignty of the sympathy–antipathy pair gives rise to all the forms of resemblance. The first three similitudes are thus all resumed and explained by it" (*OT* 25).

Some of this may seem to predict twentieth-century scientific notions such as the forces that physicists believe keep subatomic particles in their proper place and form. Foucault notes that the human body was a privileged source of analogies during the Renaissance, and quotes Pierre Belon's comparison of the skeletons of humans and birds published in 1555: "the pinion called the appendix which is in proportion to the wing and in the same place as the thumb on the hand; the extremity of the pinion which is like the fingers in us . . .; the bone given as legs to the bird corresponding to our heel" (OT 22). We might think that sympathy and antipathy seem to anticipate twentieth-century physics, and we might also think that Belon is doing comparative anatomy. Yet this is precisely the kind of thinking Foucault wants to avoid. What seems like comparative anatomy to we who are familiar with this nineteenth-century field, is in the Renaissance simply another way to demonstrate resemblances, and it is merely coincidence that these resemblances remain significant to us now. "In fact, Belon's description has no connection with anything but the positivity which, in his day, made it possible. It is neither more rational nor more scientific than an observation such as Aldrovandi's comparison of man's baser parts to the fouler parts of the world, to Hell, to the darkness of Hell, to the damned souls who are like the excrement of the Universe" (OT 22). This statement illustrates the radicalness of Foucault's historical method. He is attempting to understand the knowledge of the past in terms of its own epistemic context. To do otherwise is to assume, as do most histories of science, that humans have always been working on the same basic problems but have only recently started to come up with very many correct answers. Foucault's position holds that even when facts like the similarities between human and avian skeletons were discovered during the Renaissance, they could not have meant then what they would mean after the development of the science of comparative anatomy. What is considered truth at any given time will be determined not by its simple correspondence to a reality "out there," but by its fit into the positivities of its own day.

The system of resemblances was not explored for its own sake. On the contrary, such a project would have been impossible for the Renaissance even to imagine. But the purposes of resemblances were not always obvious, and without the proper means of interpretation they might become lost. God, however, would not allow the resemblances that he created for our benefit to remain hidden, and hence he provided "signatures" to allow us to know similitudes. Thus the sympathy of the walnut for the human head that makes walnuts a cure for head wounds and headaches, would be unknown except that the walnut looks like the brain. The reader may have noticed that this signature is itself a form of resemblance. In the Renaissance, resemblance is ubiquitous, being both visible everywhere but also invisible and therefore requiring a search. But this plethora of resemblances leads to knowledge that is both infinite and impoverished. It is infinite because there are no limits upon resemblance, and it is impoverished because it has no stability. The only link between elements of knowledge is addition. Everything is therefore equally certain but always in need of further confirmation. In this order of things, nothing new can ever be known but knowing the same thing is an infinite task (*OT* 30).

The prose of the world consists of all of the legible things, which is to say potentially all things, in nature. Among these things is language, which in the Renaissance was understood precisely to be a thing among others. Thus while we have since the classical age understood language as an arbitrary system of representation, the Renaissance understood letters, syllables, and words as having properties, and of being combined on the basis of inherent resemblances. Language is thus like the rocks, flowers, and animals of nature in all respects but this: there is one nature but many languages. Language is not perfectly revealing of its meaning because it is broken. God originally created language that was transparent and certain because it perfectly resembled the things it signified. After Babel, however, this resemblance was lost in all languages except Hebrew, which continues to reveal it at least in part. The names that Adam gave to animals, for example, have endured and carry with them the essential character of what they name. Foucault quotes Claude Duret, "Thus the stork, so greatly lauded for its charity towards its father and its mother, is called in Hebrew *Chasida*, which is to say, meek, charitable, endowed with pity . . ." (*OT* 36). One consequence of this conception of language is the privilege it gives to writing, something Foucault calls "one of the great events in Western culture" (*OT* 38). God introduced written words in the world that Adam did no more than read when he first uttered the names of the animals that bore God's marks. It was possible that before Babel and the flood there existed a form of writing composed of nature's marks and that would therefore have a power not unlike the (fictional) power we today attribute to magic words: writing something would interact with things directly.

This connection between writing and things explains two opposed characteristics of sixteenth-century knowledge. The first is the lack of distinction made between what is seen and what is read. Thus the naturalist Aldrovandi combines "exact description, reported quotations, fables without commentary, remarks dealing indifferently with an animal's anatomy, its use in heraldry, its habitat, its mythological values, or the uses to which it could be put in medicine or magic" (*OT* 39). This kind of writing would be described by the classical age natural historian Buffon as pure legend, and Foucault notes that for Aldrovandi and his contemporaries that it was all *legenda,* that is, things to be read. This is not because they privileged authority over observation, but because nature itself was "an unbroken tissue of words and signs, of accounts and characters, of discourse and forms" (*OT* 40).

The second characteristic of Renaissance knowledge deriving from the primacy of writing is the proliferation of commentary. Since nature was entirely composed of things written—not just words, but things as well—knowledge is conceived not as seeing or demonstrating, but as interpreting. The task of discovery is to give voice to the writing that is everywhere with the goal of achieving the perfect transparency of the original language. Although this goal could never be met, the project of commentary assumed a more fundamental text below the one being read that provided both a theoretical limit on interpretation and its infinite task. Thus Foucault quotes the great French essayist Montaigne: "There is more work in interpreting interpretations than in interpreting things; and more books about books than on any other subject; we do nothing but write glosses on one another" (*OT* 40). As Foucault interprets this passage, it is not about the failure of Renaissance culture, but a statement about the consequences of that culture's conception of language. Since we know that Foucault has previously complained (in *The Birth of the Clinic*) in quite similar terms about commentary in our own time, it is hard to imagine that the Renaissance plays the same more or less positive role that it had in *Madness and Civilization.* It is thus a mistake to understand *The Order of Things* as expressing a nostalgia for the Renaissance or treating it as "a mythical past, a period in which Being was still undifferentiated."[6]

Taking such a position was possible for Foucault in *Madness and Civilization* because he then held a view that took madness as the fundamental text to which all others pointed. In *The Order of Things*, however, the structures of each *episteme* are arbitrary. The Renaissance has no greater access to some essential Being than any other age. That words and things are undifferentiated in the Renaissance is if anything a weakness which he suggests modern hermeneutics repeats. The role of the Renaissance in *The Order of Things* is not prelapsarian paradise, but strange new territory that serves to disconfirm all of our assumptions about our world's history. Although we can recognize some aspects of the Renaissance *episteme* in our own time, most of us radically distinguish these from science or even knowledge. Although Foucault will argue that the break between the classical age and the modern era is as great as that between the Renaissance and the classical age, the Renaissance seems to be much more distant from our own thought. In revisiting the Renaissance with Foucault as our guide, we learn that an actual historical European culture can be as utterly different in its epistemic order as Borges's mythical taxonomy.

Representation

Representation is to the classical age what resemblance is to the Renaissance, the form all knowledge is assumed to have. Foucault shows how representation characterizes the knowledge produced by three newly formed fields, the analysis of wealth, natural history, and general grammar: "All wealth is *coinable;* and it is by this means that it enters into *circulation*—in the same way that any natural being was *characterizable,* and could thereby find its place in a *taxonomy;* that any individual was *nameable* and could find its place in an *articulated language*" (OT 175, italics in original). In each instance, a sign—the coin, the characteristic, the name—makes possible knowledge by allowing identities and differences to be established, and literally or metaphorically laid out on a table or grid. The transformation of knowledge into representation is made possible by a new understanding of the sign itself. In the Renaissance, the sign was understood as a relationship of three elements, the writing (whether natural or human), the content of that writing, and the resemblance that connected the two. In the classical age, the relationship of the sign became a binary one involving only the sign itself and the thing signified. "This new arrangement brought about the appearance of a new problem, unknown until then: in the sixteenth century, one asked oneself how it was possible to know that a sign did in fact designate what it signified; from the seventeenth century, one began to ask how a sign could be linked to what it signified" (*OT* 42–43). Thus words and things became profoundly separate, and the prose of the world came to an end.

Don Quixote marks the rupture between an *episteme* governed by resemblance and one governed by representation. Foucault argues that Cervante's novel is an extended irony of similitude where Don Quixote tries to prove the tenuous analogies between flocks, serving girls, and inns on the one hand and armies, ladies, and castles on the other and incurs only mockery as a result. "*Don Quixote* is a negative of the Renaissance world . . . resemblances and signs have dissolved their former alliance; similitudes have become deceptive and verge upon the visionary or madness" (*OT* 47). Resemblance does not disappear entirely, but it is forced to the edges of knowledge, and now will define its limits rather than its very condition. Resemblance is now a mere condition of nature, but knowledge is no longer in nature; it is the representation of nature.

There are two fundamental changes that mark the new *episteme*. First, the central task of cognition is no longer drawing things together, but discriminating among them. Thus, analysis replaces analogy as the basic intellectual procedure. Every resemblance must now be established by comparison, its truth not being accepted until its identity and differences are discovered by measurement with a common unit or by its position in an order. Furthermore, the centrality of discrimination causes history and science to become separate. The study of Plato and Aristotle is a matter of history even when they write about science, since the study of past opinions is most likely to yield disagreement. On the other hand, the direct study of things (that is, "intuition" of them) and their relations of identity and difference can produce the confident judgments of science. The second fundamental change gave science this confidence. Similitudes are now treated as finite and enumerable, and hence an entire field of knowledge could be represented by a complete census of its elements, a grid defining all possible categories, or the analysis of a sufficient number of points along an entire series. As a result, comparison can attain perfect certainty in its knowledge of identities and differences.

Given this new possibility, the classical age was able to conceive the project of a general science of order, and it is this project which gives the classical *episteme* its most characteristic emblem, the "table" or "grid" of identities and differences. Perhaps the most familiar examples of such a table are Linnaeus's tables of zoological and botanical species, but Foucault is not arguing that actual tables such as these were central to all fields of knowledge in the classical age. Rather, his claim is that knowledge produced by this *episteme* is constituted *as if* such a table were always central to it. Three forms of analysis are involved in the general science of order: *taxonomia* or classification, *genetic analysis* or chronological ordering, and *mathesis*, the science of equalities. The nexus of these three analyses of order makes possible the development of what Foucault calls three "empiricities" to distinguish them from more mathematical sciences such as physics, but also to emphasize their foundation in the visual: general grammar, natural history, and the analysis of wealth.

General grammar is the most fundamental of the three empiricities, and from it Foucault derives the basic terms of the quadrilateral, his General Table (see Figure 4) of the empirical spheres that, as we shall see, attempts to display the structure shared by each of the fields. Like natural history and the analysis of wealth, general grammar cannot be understood by reference to a modern equivalent. It is not, for example, comparative grammar, for, although comparisons are made, they are not its object. Rather, the object of general grammar is "*discourse* understood as a sequence of verbal signs" (*OT* 83). General grammar is to discourse what logic was to thought, an attempt to describe the process by which a form of representation worked. The new conception of language, which removed it from the world of things and placed it in its own separate sphere, also rendered it both completely representational and entirely transparent. Yet language and thought are not held to be identical, but rather each is regarded as a different representation, so that language becomes a representation of a representation. Thus language is not a pure expression of thought, but an analysis of it. A thought was conceived by the classical age to occur in the mind instantaneously; thoughts followed one another, but each itself occurred as a whole. Thus if one perceives that a rose is red, one perceives the redness in the rose as a whole thought. But to say that "the rose is red," one has to separate the two by putting the red after the rose. Language is then an analysis of thought, because it divides thought into component parts. Language is thus "a profound establishment of order in space. . . . General grammar is the study of verbal order in its relation to the simultaneity that it is its task to represent" (*OT* 83). But since thought can be analyzed or articulated in various ways, there must be a general grammar for each language.

The second field of knowledge Foucault takes up is natural history, which from the perspective of his interpretation is misnamed because it is the product of the division between history and science. During the Renaissance, there existed only history. Under the classical *episteme,* the one thing that natural history could not be was a history of nature. What marks the beginnings of natural history are not discoveries of new facts about nature, but what is missing from books such as Jonston's *Natural History of Quadrupeds:* the legends and fables found in the works of Renaissance naturalists are now excluded from what is proper to natural history. History in natural history is reduced to the identities and differences that are simultaneously apparent in looking at plants and animals. But besides hearsay, smell and taste are also excluded, and touch and even color are included only under the most limited conditions. What is left is the visible structure of the parts of plants or animals that consist of the following four variables: form, quantity, position and relationship, magnitude. Such analysis makes it possible to distinguish any individual specimen, but it does not provide a way to limit the description of natural objects and hence would lead to infinite comparison if not for the theory of character that defines the classes of plants and animals. There were two approaches to solving this problem, called the method and the system, respectively. The method compared the whole specimen, but only to others within an empirically constituted group that shared numerous common traits. The system selected in advance a limited number of characteristics and would study the variations and constancies of them in any individual specimen.

The relationship of character and structure produced the possibility of an exhaustive table of living beings including even living beings that were possible but not yet discovered. However, for this table to work, the meaningfulness of differences that define character must be guaranteed by repetitions in structure. If there are no identities, then differences become merely random and meaningless, and the project of natural history as a well-made language would be rendered impossible. Thus, there must be continuity in nature. In spite of the necessity of continuity, however, nature did not present itself to the observer as continuous; this required that natural history be a science and not a mere spontaneous language. The breaks and gaps in nature were explained by the effects of a chronological series of catastrophes that disarranged the earth's beings. Such a genetic analysis is then added to the taxonomy of natural history, but the chronological series is not a forerunner of evolution since the effects of time occur only outside of living beings that are themselves unchanging essences. This is true both for fixists, who argue that there are no changes in living beings as a result of these catastrophes, and for those who seem to be protoevolutionists because they believe in the advance of beings toward some goal. Such an advance does not explain the origin of species through transformation, but the continuity of nature from God to algae in which all of the variables are established in advance.

If general grammar is the theory of representation and natural history is a project in representation, the analysis of wealth is an explanation by means of representation. In the Renaissance, precious metals served as signs and measures of wealth because they were wealth. "Just as words had the same reality as what they said, just as the marks of living beings were inscribed upon their bodies in the manner of visible and positive marks, similarly, the signs that indicated wealth and measured it were bound to carry the real mark in themselves" (*OT* 169). Thus the usefulness of money depended on its intrinsic value. In the classical age, money comes to be understood as a representation rather than as something of intrinsic value. "Gold is precious because it is money—not the converse" (*OT* 176). Exchange is the process by which wealth becomes represented: "all kinds of wealth in the world are related one to another in so far as they are all part of a system of exchange" (*OT* 179).

Just as natural history constructed its table of living beings in terms of characters and structures, the analysis of wealth explained its object in terms of money and value. The theory of money was designed to explain how prices can represent different kinds of wealth. The classical age treated money as a pledge or a kind of credit, and thus as a pure fiction. Money is a conventional token, just as words are conventional signs. But this leaves money to be worth precisely the value of that which it is used to purchase, since it can always be used to obtain the same quantity of merchandise.

Like the character that can represent several individuals or classes, money can represent many things of equivalent value. But the number of entities represented by a character can be increased by simplifying it, while money can only increase what it represents by circulating faster. Therefore, the table of monetary representation must include the function of time which was excluded from the table of natural beings. Money designates wealth in relationship as it grows or diminishes over time.

The theory of value was designed to explain why people desire to exchange things. Value is a difficult issue given the assumption that for an item to be worth something it must be able to be substituted for that thing through exchange. Thus it would seem, on the one hand, that value exists in each object before it is exchanged, so that each trader gains and loses equal value. But on the other hand, what each person needs in order to live has no value because it cannot be exchanged, and what he does not need to live has no value until it is exchanged. Thus the classical age produced two theories of value, one that analyzed value as a function of exchange, and the other that treated value as a prior condition of exchange. The groups who held these two positions were named the physiocrats and the utilitarians, and they are usually depicted as entirely antithetical to each other. But just as the system and the method in natural history share the same conditions of possibility, so the physiocrats and utilitarians also are a product of the same *episteme*.

Foucault summarizes his treatment of the classical *episteme* as follows:

. . . for Classical thought, systems of natural history and theories of money or trade have the same conditions of possibility as language itself. This means two things: first, that order in nature and order in the domain of wealth have the same mode of being, for the Classical experience, as the order of representations as manifested by words; second, that words form a system of signs sufficiently privileged, when it is a question of revealing the order of things, for natural history—if it is well organized—and money—if it is well regulated—to function in the same way as language. (*OT* 203)

What are the consequences of this elaborate analysis of ancient and largely forgotten modes of thought? They are not always stated as prominently as we might like, but they are enormous. The classical age has a special significance for our own era's history of itself. Thus we may recognize without much difficulty philosophers such as Bacon and Descartes when Foucault depicts them as warning of the illusions of resemblance. We have long recognized the period Foucault is describing here as the Age of Reason, marked by the end of illusions, superstitions, and magic, but Foucault believes that although the new epistemological formation could be called "rationalism," such a designation does not go deep enough to reach the structural level that, he argues, makes possible not only the particular knowledge that the age will produce, but also the very conditions that pertain when something is known (*OT* 56). But what Foucault does not state, however, is that by attributing the character of classical knowledge to a deep structural arrangement of terms, he is depriving rationalism of its rational character. Reason now becomes a historical accident, the product of a structural realignment over which it had no control. Foucault also disputes two other traditional characterizations of classical thought, mechanism and mathematicization, which he argues reflect only partial or temporary consistencies within it. What is at stake, then, is the entire history of modern science which, as it is usually written, has its origin in reason, mechanism, and mathematicization. Each of these explanations serves the self-interest of modern science, and misses what is in fact definitive of knowledge in the classical age.

Foucault achieves his rewriting of the classical age by his emphasis on language, which enables *The Order of Things* to become an even more powerful attack on positivism than was *The Birth of the Clinic*. By calling our attention to the importance of language in the classical *episteme,* Foucault is able to reduce both mechanism and mathematicization to the level of subsidiary elements in the larger project of the general science of order, or *mathesis*. This rewriting of what before Foucault was called the history of ideas has the potential to alter our entire conception of the development of science and Western culture. The traditional histories take the mathematicization of nature as one of several major innovations that permit modern science to come into being. In *The Birth of the Clinic*, we saw Foucault disputing another of these supposed innovations, the return to observation. In *The Order of Things* he argues that naming is more fundamental than counting in the classical *episteme,* and that algebra can be understood as a form of naming. Thus modern science stems not from fundamental changes in mathematics or its application, but from changes in language.

Measurement, one aspect of *mathesis*, did of course make expanded use of mathematics, but another aspect of *mathesis* was the system of signs, and it is this development which gives rise to new forms of knowledge that do not rely on mechanism or mathematicization, including general grammar, natural history, and the analysis of wealth. These fields are usually ignored by the history of science, and we might safely guess they are ignored because they do not fit the official pattern.

By placing order rather than mathematics at the center of the classical *episteme*, Foucault gives new unity to the knowledge of that period, but in so doing he undermines positivism's claims to having discovered mathematics as the key to nature's truth. He does this in a way which is more powerful than, although dependent upon, the phenomenological critique of Edmund Husserl who showed that geometry did not deal with natural shapes, but with human "ideal-izations."[7] It is also more effective than the critique of the dehumanizing effects of mechanism found in Frankfurt school philosophers such as Theodor Adorno and Jürgen Habermas.[8] The strength of Foucault's argument is that it provides an alternative history, where the phenomenological analysis merely points out a philosophical mistake and the Frankfurt School critique, even more weakly, complains about the effects of modern science. Foucault directly attacks one of the most cherished myths of origin, an origin in the return to the pure truth of seeing and the natural language of mathematics, and replaces it with a history that locates a new way of seeing in an arbitrary structural configuration.

A second major result of Foucault's rewriting of the history of science is the recognition that the division of knowledge into separate fields or disciplines has a distinct historical beginning, helping us to realize that these fields themselves are cultural constructions and not the transparent duplication of nature. This division will in the nineteenth century produce the modern disciplines, but eighteenth-century fields of knowledge cannot be understood by reading modern disciplines back into them. Thus Foucault's project is the recovery of the specific past fields of study that the history of science has forgotten. Complex objects of study such as "life," "nature," or "man" do not "present themselves to the curiosity of knowledge spontaneously and passively" for they are not natural objects like rocks or trees, but are constituted by the disciplines themselves (*OT* 72). Thus we cannot take our own categories of knowledge and seek to discover how earlier periods understood them, for in the earlier periods these categories simply did not exist. Foucault's notion of the *episteme* and his analysis of classical fields of knowledge give grounds for what he merely assumed in *Madness and Civilization:* the radical alterity of the past.

Foucault's account of the classical *episteme* makes clear what is obscured by the disorientation we feel in the face of the Renaissance *episteme:* the degree to which structuralism continues to make its presence felt in Foucault's thought. In choosing representation as the distinguishing feature of the classical *episteme,* Foucault gives the period a character that can be emblematized by the table, just as mechanism gave the period the clock as its emblem. But Foucault is not content to describe classical thought at a level of generality that could be confused with approaches from the history of ideas he is trying to leave behind. So he asserts that the classical *episteme* is structured by the terms used during that period to designate the elements of discursive representation as formulated by general grammar. By taking relations between these terms to be constitutive of natural history and the analysis of wealth, Foucault treats the theories of these fields as the inevitable products of various combinations of the terms or of the ones particular to the individual field.

As a graphic representation of the centrality Foucault gives to the structure of articulation and attribution, designation and derivation, one should consult Foucault's own General Table. This table shows how general grammar, natural history, and the analysis of wealth are structured in the classical age, and how that structure shifts in the nineteenth century to produce philology, biology, and economics. Foucault's quadrilateral is similar to Greimas's semiotic rectangle, like Lévi-Strauss's triangle, another important structuralist way of picturing relationships between ideas. Greimas's rectangle (Figure 3) starts from an opposition between two terms, a proposition and its contradiction. It then adds to this binary opposition, the contrary of each of the first two terms.

If one were attempting to analyze a cultural practice, sexual relations for example, one might fill in the positions as follows: A stands for prescribed behavior or matrimonial relations; B for prohibited behavior—for example, incest; not B for behavior not pro-

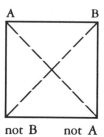

Figure 3. Greimas's Semiotic Rectangle, where B is the contradiction of A

hibited—male adultery; and not A for behavior not prescribed—female adultery.[9]

The layout of the Foucault's diagram (Figure 4) differs from Greimas's in that the points of contradiction are diagonally opposed to each other, while the contrary relations are expressed by the solid lines on opposing sides of the rectangle. The quadrilateral differs further in that it is depicted in a diamond shape standing as it were on one of its corners. Foucault's scheme appears more complicated than Greimas's because no term is represented as fixed in any one of the four positions, so that there does not seem at first to be any contradiction involved among these positions. In fact, Foucault's description of the quadrilateral relates each of the four elements to each of the others in terms of both opposition and support. Thus each quadrilateral shows four different semiotic rectangles imposed on each other. There is, however, a primary one.

The quadrilateral begins as semiotic rectangle in which the proposition, or attribution as Foucault calls it in the diagram, is itself in the position of proposition, while designation is its contradiction. Articulation then becomes the contrary of attribution, and derivation the contrary of designation. Attribution is the positive statement because it is the minimal requirement needed for discourse. "A proposition exists—and discourse too—when we affirm the existence of an attributive link between two things, when we say that this *is* that" (*OT* 94, italics in original). What contradicts proposition or judgment is indication, or designation. While a proposition takes the form of "*x* is *y*," a name points something out, designating it from among other things that could be indicated. The theory of designation traced words back to what were thought to be their roots in primitive cries which merely indicated the object named

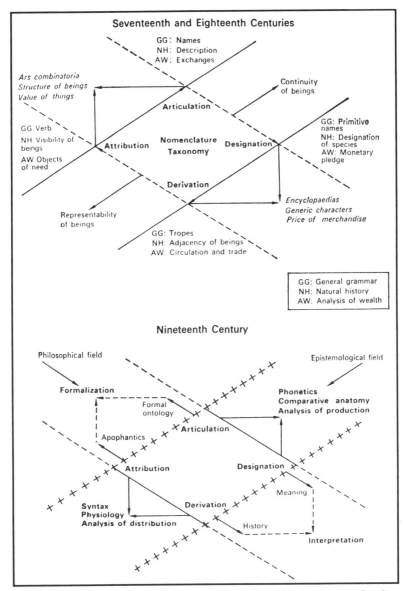

Figure 4. Reprinted from Foucault's *The Order of Things: An Archaeology of the Human Sciences,* trans. Alan Sheridan (New York: Pantheon, 1970), 201, by permission of Random House.

and which are not discourse. Another bit of evidence that supports the interpretation of attribution and designation as contradictory is the way these two terms figure in Foucault's treatment of natural history and the analysis of wealth. Each of these fields is structured mainly by a single binary opposition, structure versus character and value versus money, respectively. On the table, Foucault makes each of these a function of two terms, so that structure and value are placed between attribution and articulation, and character and money are placed between designation and derivation. But in each case the contrary term is spurious. Natural historical character and monetary price are forms of designation, as Foucault's own language shows. Value and structure are fundamentally judgments; they are attributions of objects.

It can be safely asserted that the General Table is not one of Foucault's rhetorical successes. Although it has not generally been criticized, it has been ignored. This is at least partially the result of its failure to simplify the complexities of the discussion. A diagram should not be harder to comprehend than the language that it is supposed to illustrate. Another and more significant problem is Foucault's use of the terms borrowed from general grammar. He fails to persuade us that these terms represent the structural limitations of knowledge during both the classical age and modern periods because they remain so foreign to the actual discourses themselves. It is hard here not to understand Foucault as performing some sort of commentary in which the deep truth of classical and perhaps modernist knowledge turns out to be the relations among these terms, yet this would contradict Foucault's self-understanding of his project. The quadrilateral is useful as an illustration of Foucault's relations with structuralism. What distinguishes Foucault's thought from simple structuralism is the fact that he does not treat his terms as contradictions but instead "deconstructs" as it were the oppositions by showing that the terms contain each other, make each other possible. What constitutes his continuing link with structuralism in *The Order of Things* is his assumption that the relations between a set of terms define the structure of knowledge within a given period, and that a shift in these relations will mark a major cultural change. Thus just as the shifting relations among terms marked the mutation of discourse in *The Birth of the Clinic,* the shifting relations among terms will mark the mutation of the classical *episteme* into the modern.

Man and His Disappearance

Resemblance and representation each describes a conception of the relation of a sign to what it signifies. The shift in the Western *episteme* from the Renaissance to the classical age is defined by a change from one conception to the other. This change is a relatively straightforward choice between two halves of a binary opposition. The next epistemic shift cannot be correlated with any such clear structural change. Foucault tries to suggest that it can be by using the General Table to depict the modern *episteme* as a function of a new set of relations between the same terms that defined the classical age. Yet these terms never play an important role in Foucault's treatment of the modern period. Instead, it is the figure of man that serves as the emblem for the modern *episteme*, producing the strange series, "resemblance, representation, man," as the chronology of the Western *episteme*. How does this non sequitur come about?

One major change in knowledge since the Renaissance was the proliferation of separate fields. In the modern era these fields continue to grow exponentially. If it was harder for Foucault to successfully convey his sense of what classical empiricities shared than it was for him to characterize Renaissance knowledge, it will be still harder to bring together the numerous modern disciplines that begin to develop in the nineteenth century. What distinguishes the modern *episteme*, then, is not the form knowledge takes—it will take different forms, although representation remains the major one—but the problem knowledge is centered on. The area of knowledge Foucault is dealing with will cover a smaller percentage of the whole, for the modern *episteme* is not asserted to support physics or mathematics, which were at least related to the classical *episteme* through *mathesis*. The human sciences of which *The Order of Things* is an archaeology actually come into being in the modern era, and they are defined by a new object of investigation, man himself.

The shift from representation to man is not so illogical as it at first seems, especially if one remembers the problem already expressed in *Las Meninas* of the impossibility of representing the observer of a representation: "In Classical thought, the personage for whom the representation exists, and who represents himself within it, recognizing himself therein as an image or reflection, he who ties together all the interlacing threads of the 'representation in the form of a picture or table'—he is never to be found in that table himself. Before the end of the eighteenth century, *man* did not exist" (*OT* 308, italics in original). Thus *man* was absent from the classical *episteme*, but he is a present absence, an absence that structures, as in *Las Meninas*. But to say that "man did not exist" is, if not illogical, surely one of the most striking reversals of Foucault's thought. Even if we are quite aware that Foucault does not mean that the species Homo sapiens had not yet evolved on earth, we still are likely to react in disbelief. How can Foucault say that man did not exist prior to 200 years ago?

We assume that man has existed as long as there have been human beings because of our assumption that human nature is a biological or metaphysical constant. It was Foucault's lifelong project to overturn this assumption. For Foucault, human nature is always the construction of a particular culture at a particular time. Human nature during the modern period is different from what it was in the classical age, but also the meaning of "human nature" differs between the two. Under the classical *episteme*, human nature itself prohibited any science of man. During this period, human nature was interwoven with nature by the mechanism of knowledge, and man "does not occupy a place in nature through the intermediary of the regional, limited, specific 'nature' that is granted . . . to all other beings as a birthright" (*OT* 310). Thus natural history, general grammar, and the analysis of wealth could not define man, because he could not appear on their tables. Man appears when biology, philology, and economics articulate laws that govern the individual, but that are also capable of being completely known to that individual. Man is the "being whose nature (that which determines it, contains it, and has traversed it from the beginning of time) is to know nature, and itself, in consequence, as a natural being" (*OT* 310).

Man does not appear on the scene suddenly at the start of the modern period. His possibility is the product of a two-stage development, the first stage of which does appear with some suddenness between 1775 and 1795. The major epistemic shift that permits biology, economics, and philosophy to exist is that historical succession replaces simultaneous order. Knowledge, which the classical *episteme* had constituted as spatial and visible, was now conceived as temporal and invisible. History has been associated with nineteenth-century thought just as reason has been associated with the classical age. Characteristically, Foucault does not focus on changes that explicitly historicized knowledge, but on those that rendered it invisible. In the first stage of the mutation that brought about the modern *episteme,* economics, biology, and philology continue to constitute their domains as representations, but in each case there is introduced an invisible element that serves to undermine representation.

In economics, that element is labor, which is invisible in the sense that although it is the measure of all wealth (and as a measure, still a representation), people do not perceive it to be an object of exchange: "As men experience things . . . what they are exchanging is what is 'indispensable, commodious or pleasurable' to them, but for the economist, what is actually circulating in the form of things is labor—not objects of need representing one another, but time and toil, transformed, concealed, forgotten" (*OT* 224–25). Similarly, biologists of this first stage—during which Lamarck named the discipline—discovered organic structure and substituted it for the visible structure that had been used by natural historians. Organic structure was identified by characteristics that were not visible but were essential to a class, so that one biologist could argue that alimentary functions are the most important because they account for relations between many different parts of an animal. Organic structure also entailed the divorce of nomenclature from classification in that nomenclature must continue to depend on visible traits, and thus it forecasts the end of the preeminence of taxonomy. Language analysis follows this same pattern of mutation, albeit more slowly, perhaps because it is more strongly linked to representation than the other two fields. But in the early nineteenth century, language came to be understood as having a formal structure that could be studied apart from its representative function. Languages came to be compared based on differences in inflectional systems or in sounds and their relations and transformations. During the classical age, the history of a language was determined by what it represented; now "there is an interior 'mechanism' in languages which determines not only each one's individuality but also its resemblances to the others" (*OT* 236). Thus an interior element in each field undermines the order defined by representation and makes history necessary.

This is not to say that the classical empiricities had no sense of a past. Each did account for something like history, but not as history. Instead of events and developments, each field understood the past as an unbroken continuity or succession. Thus general grammar assumed a continuous series of derivations and externally introduced modifications that reached all the way back to a prelinguistic origin. Natural history depicted the march of living beings through preordained variations. The analysis of wealth treated history as the cyclical alternation of periods of poverty and riches. What is missing in each case is anything of which one could write a history, for the changes that time might yield are either totally random or repetitious. What the first stage of the modern *episteme* does is to provide a motive force that will drive change in each domain: labor, life, and language. "Thus, European culture is inventing for itself a depth in which what matters is no longer identities, distinctive characters, permanent tables with all their possible paths and routes, but great hidden forces developed on the basis of their primitive and inaccessible nucleus, origin, causality, and history" (*OT* 251). It is the invisible which is the source of temporality.

Foucault focuses on one figure who he believes marks the full transformation of the Western *episteme* into its modern form in each of three areas. In economics, Ricardo changed labor from what had been the measure of wealth, a form of representation, in Adam Smith into production, that is, the source of all value. This change introduces history into economics because value is determined by conditions of production that have been brought into existence. In economics, unlike biology or philology, history not only describes the past but projects a future. The development that Ricardo predicts is a gradual slowing down to a stasis, which is in effect the end of history. Marx also projects the end of history, not as stasis, but as a reversal that will inaugurate an entirely new history. Foucault argues that Ricardo and Marx represent merely two alternatives offered by the fundamental epistemic shift of which Ricardo is the first indication.

Cuvier establishes biology by elevating function over structure in the analysis of organs. This change allows organs within an animal to be understood in relations of coexistence, hierarchy, and dependence with each other, where the classical age saw organs only in terms of their taxonomic efficacy. "From Cuvier onward, it is life in its non-perceptible, purely functional aspect that provides the basis for the exterior possibility of a classification. The classification of living beings is no longer to be found in the great expanse of order; the possibility of classification now arises from the depths of life" (*OT* 268). It is life in its functional aspect as well, that provides a history of nature, but such history does not come about until evolution provides a theory of the relations between life and its environment. But, according to Foucault, the possibility of this theory rests on the prior invention of biology, the study of life.

Bopp developed a new theory of the root that radically altered the way in which linguistic change and the relationships between languages were understood. Verbs and personal pronouns, rather than *to be* and proper nouns, are understood as the primordial elements of language. The roots of these verbs express wishes, desires, processes, and actions, and thus "language is 'rooted' not in the things perceived, but in the active subject" (*OT* 290). Language changes are therefore now perceived to result not from above or outside, but from below, from an *energia,* a ceaseless activity internal to language. This perception leads to a new understanding of the relationships between languages. They are now divided into broad groupings that are discontinuous in relation to one another. The creation of these groups proceeds from the possibility of direct, lateral comparison of languages that does not need to account for elements shared by all languages or the representative stock on which they draw. The historicity of languages is thus like that of living beings in that each develops multiple variations within discontinuous groups. Sanskrit, Greek, Latin, and the Germanic languages are shown to be fraternally related to each other and derived from a common ancestor, just as different species of animals may evolve from a single species.

One result of this new treatment of language is that it becomes once again an object like other objects and no longer the privileged form of knowledge itself. But Foucault notes that there are what he calls "compensations" for this "demotion" of language. First, since scientific knowledge must be expressed in language, there developed the projects of creating a perfectly transparent language that would be a copy of nature and of the search for a logic independent of language, symbolic logic. Second, the study of language was held to be of critical value because language now was the carrier of tradition, of habits of thought, of hidden memory. Thus there was a revival of exegesis that Foucault finds at the heart of major modern figures such as Marx, Nietzsche, and Freud. Third, there is the appearance of literature as a distinct form of language. Literature is philology's double, its twin rival which takes language away from grammar to the naked power of speech.

If Foucault had relatively little to say about philosophy in the classical age, it is because, to state it as a Foucauldian reversal, philosophy did not exist. There were, of course, people such as Locke and Descartes who called themselves philosophers, but they were concerned with problems of representation and worked at the same level of analysis as those dealing with wealth, general grammar, or living beings. What we have meant by philosophy since the nineteenth century is an enterprise devoted to theories of meaning and epistemology. The importance of the splitting off of different knowledges now becomes clear, for philosophy emerges as a result of the withdrawal of representation as the common ground of all knowledge. As a result, philosophy takes up under the name of epistemology the job of finding a ground for knowledge.[10] Thus Foucault's archaeology finds itself confronted with another class of artifacts that have no direct ancestors in the classical age, but together they reveal the birth of Man.

Man is defined by three philosophical problems that Foucault characterizes as "doubles" since each consists of an oscillating pair of terms. Each of the doubles is an aspect of the individual's dual role "as an object of knowledge and as a subject that knows" (OT 312). The general attempt to think man, Foucault calls the analytic of finitude. Finitude is not the sudden discovery of human mortality, but the problem of founding knowledge once representation has become a problem having lost its transparency and its guarantee in God-given human nature. During the classical age, humans like other beings had their place on the table, but it was not necessary for them to make representation possible. Finitude becomes epistemologically significant only when knowledge must be founded on the human subject. Previously, God and the transparency of representation provided an infinite ground for the truth of perception. Now representation and knowledge are made possible by a finite being, whose finitude is announced over and over again by the factual limitations that are everyday being discovered by the empiricities. Man becomes "an individual who lives, speaks, and works in accordance with the laws of an economics, a philology, and a biology, but who also, by a sort of internal torsion and overlapping, has acquired the right, through the interplay of those very laws, to know them and to subject them to total clarification" (OT 310). This analytic of finitude produces the doubles that constitute man.

The first double is the empirical and the transcendental. The distinction comes from Kant who hoped to guarantee empirical knowledge by founding it on the transcendental form of knowledge. No stable division between these two aspects of knowledge can be maintained, however, because the forms are, by the nature of Kant's critical philosophy, always about to be explained by the empirical. Truth itself becomes divided: "there must, in fact, exist a truth that is of the same order as the object—the truth that is . . . expressed through the body and the rudiments of perception . . . that appears as illusions are dissipated, and as history establishes disalientated status for itself; but there must also exist a truth that is of the order of discourse—a truth that makes it possible to employ . . . a language that will be true" (*OT* 320). This second truth, the truth of discourse, is the locus of the instability of the empirical and the transcendental: "either this true discourse finds its foundation and model in the empirical truth whose genesis in nature and in history it retraces, so that one has an analysis of the positivist type . . . or the true discourse anticipates the truth whose nature and history it defines; it sketches it out in advance and foments it from a distance, so that one has a discourse of the eschatological type" (*OT* 320). Comte, the positivist philosopher, and Marx represent examples of these two positions. Comtean positivism renders this true discourse as a reduction, while Marxism makes it a promise. In either case, the empirical and the transcendental merge as one takes over the other. Thus, according to Foucault, modern thought has been doomed to search endlessly for a way to keep the empirical and the transcendental separate, and the only way to end this futile effort is to question the existence of man.

The double of the *cogito* and the unthought is a product of the conditions imposed on the human subject by the empirical/transcendental double. If man's knowledge is known through the empirical conditions of his existence, then he cannot be the transparent "I think" that Descartes thought him to be. The modern *episteme* turns Descartes on his feet, and holds that "I am, therefore I think" because the one who thinks is always the same one who exists empirically and historically, who lives a life that cannot be entirely thought. This remainder is the unthought, that indispensable element of human being that is always out of the reach of one's thought. Its most familiar name may be the one Freud gave it, the unconscious, but it was not discovered by Freud but was born with man. Hegel called it the *for-itself;* Marx dubbed it *alienated man.* Foucault suggests, however, that the unthought is in fact the Other, and is therefore mistakenly sought in man's nature or history, when it in fact exists outside of man, as a twin or shadow. Thus, just as modern thought is caught in an endless search for a way to separate the empirical and the transcendental, it is also forced to try to know its own shadow, only to discover again and again that the shadow moves with every attempt to bring light to bear on it.

The transcendental and the *cogito* are two ways that knowledge might be founded. A third is the discovery of the origin of knowledge. The third double Foucault calls the retreat and return of the origin. In the classical age the origin was the place where representation was most nearly duplication. Thus, the analysis of wealth conceived of barter as its origin because in barter the representations one made of one's own and the other's property were equivalent. Language had its origin in primitive naming and the language of action, the cry or the gesture. But these were not historical events in the modern sense, but rather mythologies of a prehistoric time that explained the current situation. In the modern age, language, labor, and life acquire their own historicities. Thus, for example, "the origin of language becomes a genuinely historical question. The beginnings of language are shrouded in mystery and retreat further and further into the past in the face of empirical investigation."[11] The retreat of the origin is the recession of the historical beginnings of knowledge deeper and deeper into history. Yet human beings must know that history since they willy-nilly communicate and labor and live. But they know without knowing that they know. Thus the founding practices that enable each field of knowledge also retreat before the quest. Since the origin cannot be reached in the past, it becomes "what thought has yet to think" (*OT* 332). But here again the origin recedes, since this promise is also empty. Here again man's finitude is discovered, and again this finitude in the form of the unattainable origin is asserted to provide a transcendental escape precisely because it cannot be attained, that is, known empirically.

Foucault's project to construct an archaeology of the human sciences, psychology, sociology, and literary and cultural studies, can now be completed. The human sciences emerge in a niche created when the modern *episteme* made more or less positive sciences of labor, life, and language, and made man out of the crisis of representation. Psychology, sociology, and literary and cultural studies are not, then, the result of the discovery of neglected fields "already outlined, perhaps surveyed as a whole, but allowed to lie fallow, which it was then their task to elaborate with positive methods and with concepts that had at last become scientific" (*OT* 344). Rather, these fields are defined and become possible only under the specific configuration of the modern *episteme*. Foucault pictures the human sciences as situated inside a three-dimensional space created by the three other forms of modern knowledge: on one plain, the physical sciences and mathematics; on the second, the empirical sciences of life, labor, and language; on the third, philosophical reflection. The human sciences are related to each of these plains of knowledge by borrowing from them and commenting on them, but remain, as it were, unfixed, free to roam around. They represent a danger to the other fields signified by such terms as "psychologism." The human sciences themselves are notoriously unstable; their instability results not from the density of their object or their metaphysical status or the transcendental character of man, but from their precarious relations to the epistemological configuration in which they exist (*OT* 348).

At the beginning of the chapter I observed that Foucault did not disparage the thought of the *epistemes* he discussed. While this is strictly the case with the Renaissance and classical *epistemes*, Foucault becomes more critical in dealing with the modern period. As Dreyfus and Rabinow note, he cannot say that the modern sciences of man are true or that they are mistaken because he believes that what counts as the truth is determined by the discursive practice of a particular discipline. But Foucault does criticize discourse about man as leading to "warped" and "twisted" forms of thought (*OT* 343). Furthermore, this discourse is disintegrating as the oscillation between the doubles begins to seem either boring or discouraging.[12] The predicted disappearance of man will result from this disintegration. What will replace man and form the problematic of a new *episteme* remains only vaguely suggested in *The Order of Things*, but his criticisms make it clear that Foucault welcomes this rupture, that he is among those who find man no longer of interest except as an artifact. Nietzsche, whose proclamation of the death of God, for Foucault, heralds the end of his murderer, is the first prophet of the new *episteme*. Psychoanalysis and ethnology are seen as anticipating it to a certain extent while not escaping the confines of the modern. The most important marker is the return of language to the unity that it lost at the end of the classical age. Such a unity is marked by linguistics as "a pure theory of language which would provide the ethnology and the psychoanalysis thus conceived with their formal model. . . . In linguistics, one would have a science perfectly founded in the order of positivities exterior to man . . . [and which] would appear to traverse, animate, and disturb the whole constituted field of the human sciences" (*OT* 381). Language is thus the problematic that Foucault sees as replacing man. At least in part this judgment is based upon the fact that the problematic of man had meant the end of an earlier problematic of language.

> For the entire modern *episteme*—that which was formed towards the end of the eighteenth century and still serves as the positive ground of our knowledge, that which constituted man's particular mode of being and the possibility of knowing him empirically—that entire *episteme* was bound up with the disappearance of Discourse and its featureless reign, with the shift of language towards objectivity, and with its reappearance in multiple form. If this same language is now emerging with greater and greater insistence in a unity that we ought to think but cannot as yet do so, is this not the sign that the whole of this configuration is now about to topple, and that man is in the process of perishing as the being of language continues to shine ever brighter upon our horizon? Since man was constituted at a time when language was doomed to dispersion, will he not be dispersed when language regains its unity? (*OT* 385–86)

The original title of *The Order of Things* was "The Archaeology of Structuralism."[13] In the last pages of the book, it becomes clear how *The Order of Things* could still merit that description. Structuralism is precisely a system which takes pure language as a formal model for other disciplines. And in so far as the Foucault of *The Order of Things* could be considered a structuralist, the book might be read as an extended justification for his own work. Yet Foucault discarded the original title, and in the foreword to the English edition he describes commentators who have labeled him a structuralist as "half-witted" (*OT* xiv). Foucault may have decided that if structuralism were an expression of a new *episteme*, then he could not write its archaeology, but he may also have changed his mind about the importance of structuralism. Thus *The Order of Things* achieves not the description, much less the founding, of a new order, but rather the analysis and destabilizing of an old one. Since Foucault admits that our knowledge remains grounded in the modern *episteme*, the forecast of a new *episteme* can be no more than a guess, and the shape of the *episteme* cannot be known. Nevertheless, Foucault believes we may be certain that man is an object of fairly recent invention and is not likely to long be the center of our attention: "man is neither the oldest nor the most constant problem that has been posed for human knowledge" (*OT* 386).

Foucault and the History of Science

It would be impossible to summarize in this volume the vast commentary on *The Order of Things*. It seems useful, however, to explore briefly the differences between Foucault's version of the history of a field and the standard reading of its history. As a matter of convenience, I will focus on biology. Foucault's rediscovery of the project of general grammar provides a common foundation upon which to build the description of the other two sciences. But because its history is relatively obscure, Foucault's version of that history is likely to trouble relatively few readers. On the other hand, his discussions of natural history and the analysis of wealth constitute a rewriting of the histories of biology and economics that has produced opposition from those quarters. It is quite difficult, however, to determine a "standard" history of economics, especially given the split between Marxist and capitalist economists. Biology is a more unified discipline and it also has a well-developed body of historical writing devoted to it.

Since modern biology is governed by what Kuhn might call the Darwinian paradigm, one might well expect to find much of the history of pre-Darwinian times focused on ideas that seem to anticipate evolution. In this writing, Lamarck is seen as representing the break with premodern thought, with thinkers such as Diderot and Bonnet, who are said to have a "presentiment" of life's transformative power, as forerunners. These latter thinkers were opposed during their own time by Linnaeus and others who believed in the external fixity of the species. According to Foucault, this classical-age conflict is misread by modern historians. Both positions in the conflict are made possible by the same structures that govern the classical age, so neither is any more advanced or modern than the other. This exposes another major consequence of the notion of the *episteme*, its flattening out of conflicts within a period. In Foucault's reading of the history of science, major changes do not occur as the result of one camp winning out over another. Any given *episteme* will always produce several opposing positions that are entirely internal to it. Thus the argument over mobility versus fixity of species is internal to the classical *episteme*. Biology was produced not by one of these camps winning over the other, but by a change in epistemic conditions external to both of them. This perspective allows Foucault to credit Cuvier, a fixist, with originating modern biology by taking up anatomy and dissection. Modern biology is defined by the concept of life, not by evolution.

This view of the history of biology is unusual, although not without support from others such as Georges Canguilhem. As a principle of analysis, however, the disregard of conflicts within a given period of a science's history finds support from Kuhn's notion that paradigms change not as a result of progress made under a paradigm, but as the result of anomalies produced by that paradigm.[14] Foucault does not offer any explanation for why *epistemes* change, so we cannot link him with Kuhn too closely on this point. However, both thinkers do reject the view that sees scientists as moving ever closer to the truth by consistently working to solve theoretical problems by testing theories and eliminating the false ones. Rather, each proposes a picture in which new constructs—paradigms or *epistemes*—precede the production of new facts or new forms of knowledge. The most general critique by biologists of Foucault has been focused on his periodizing, rather than the *episteme* as a concept or his specific account of any particular period. Ernst Mayr, for example, in his definitive history of biology, *The Growth of Biological Thought,* argues that periodization may accurately describe the physical sciences but not biology, which has developed differently in different countries and often with conflicting traditions within those countries.[15] On the other hand, Mayr regards Cuvier as perhaps the most important pre-Darwinian biologist who "produced more new knowledge that ultimately supported the theory of evolution" than any one else.[16] John C. Greene, in a review of *The Order of Things,* criticizes Foucault's interpretation of the historical significance of each of the major figures of eighteenth-century natural history. Greene's interpretation places the revolution in thought as occurring precisely between the static and evolutionary views of nature, the latter being prefigured by Buffon and articulated by Lamarck.[17] Greene's view of Lamarck is no more orthodox than Foucault's is of Cuvier, but the terms of Greene's history are thoroughly in keeping with the orthodoxy of modern biology. Evolution is, like Christ in the Christian reading of history, the event toward which everything before it points, and from which everything after follows.

One might argue that modern biology must write its history this way, and that it would take a nonbiologist like Foucault to perceive the possibility of a more fundamental change that allowed evolution to come to prominence. In fact, Foucault does argue something like this when he calls his own work "fiction" in the sense that it lies outside of contemporary discursive formations that determine what shall be considered true (*PK* 193). In placing himself in this position vis-à-vis the established disciplines, Foucault renders himself unassailable. The charges that historians or practitioners of these fields might make against his work are already discounted in advance as the products of discursive regimes, or at least discursive formations other than his own. Thus he forestalls the repeated complaints that his work gets the historical facts wrong, or that his work—at least through *The Order of Things*—takes most of its examples and evidence from France, but makes claims about all of Western culture.[18] But, of course, these complaints are only neutralized if one accepts Foucault's general assumptions. They continue to carry weight within the disciplines that produce them. This situation itself seems to confirm the picture of knowledge and its relation to power that Foucault will develop in the work that follows *The Order of Things* in that the argument between Foucault and his critics can only be settled by the relative social and political power of one position over another. Even if we do not want to go all the way with Foucault's rejection of reason as the arbiter of intellectual disputes, it can still be maintained that the import of Foucault's conception of the history of *epistemes* will not stand or fall on the basis of factual accuracy or inaccuracy. Only larger or more fundamental arguments about knowledge and history can decide this issue.

Chapter Five
Archaeology and Genealogy

In 1963, in the same year as *The Birth of the Clinic,* Foucault published *Death and the Labyrinth: The World of Raymond Roussel* (the title of the French edition was simply *Raymond Roussel*).[1] This book has always been regarded as an anomaly in Foucault's oeuvre, even though his other literary essays on such figures as Georges Bataille and Maurice Blanchot have not. This is undoubtedly the result of Roussel's lack of reputation or readership in France or anywhere else. Furthermore, while the other literary essays deal with themes such as transgression and the origins of literature, *Death and the Labyrinth* is mainly a work of explication—one might even call it a reader's guide—that advances no major arguments about larger issues. A reader's guide to an unread poet and novelist is not likely to attract much attention. But Roussel is clearly an important figure in Foucault's conception of twentieth-century literature and may be regarded as an important element of the background of Foucault's own thought.

In *The Order of Things,* Foucault cites Roussel, along with the dramatist Artaud, as one who heralds a "new mode of being of literature" in which language itself becomes not merely what the writing is about, but which it is about in such a way that literature itself is dehumanized. This literature takes up the fundamental forms of finitude, but in doing so leads us not to the heart of man, but to "the brink of that which limits him . . . where death prowls, where thought is extinguished, where the promise of the origin interminably recedes. . . . In Roussel's work, language, having been reduced to powder by a systematically fabricated chance, recounts interminably the repetition of death and the enigma of divided origins" (*OT* 383). "Systematically fabricated chance" describes Roussel's work accurately and the phrase also reveals the connection between Roussel and Foucault's other work. Roussel's poems and novels might be likened to extremely complicated puzzles or word games. They are mechanical constructions deriving from a rigid and purely arbitrary system established in advance of the writing. Thus words, put through a mill, become like powder. They do not lose their meanings, but their meanings and even their possibility of meaning is irrelevant to Roussel's project. It is this irrelevance of meaning that heralds the death of man.

Let us consider several of Roussel's text machines. His book *Impressions of Africa* has its origin in the words *billard* (billiard table) and *pillard* (plunderer). Roussel would choose two nearly identical words and then add similar words designed to produce two different meanings, creating two sentences identical except for the minute differences in the original two words. *Billard* and *pillard* yield *les lettres du blanc sur les bandes du vieux billard* (the white letters on the cushions of the old billiard table) and *les lettres du blanc sur les bandes du vieux pillard* (the white man's letters on the hordes of the old plunderer). The novel is about a shipwrecked European who is captured by a black chieftain. He sends his wife letters describing battles and cannibalism, with the chieftain as hero. The first sentence not only gives rise to the second, but to much else as well. As Roussel himself explains, "I sought new words related to the word *billard*, always with the intention of using them in a sense other than the obvious one, and each time something new was created. Thus *queue* (billiard cue/train) provided [the plunderer] Talou's robes with a train."[2] Neither sentence, however, actually appears in the novel. We know about them only because Roussel wrote a book entitled *How I Wrote Certain of My Books*. Foucault notes that there are two levels at work here. At the deepest level, that of the billiard table, there is a coherence built on association. But at the next level, the elements generated are foreign to one another since they are related to the first level only as homonyms. As Foucault explains, "the game consists in retracing the distance produced by the dispersion of a sentence reduced to its homonyms, independent of any coherent meaning" (*DL* 35).

A second of Roussel's devices is if anything more arbitrary since in it the homonyms do not form a sentence but merely a sequence of words that sound like the words of the generating sentence. The sentence *"J'ai du bon tabac dans ma tabatière"* (I've got good tobacco in my tobacco pouch) yields *"Jade, tube, onde, aubade en mat à basse tierce"* (jade, tube, water, mat object, to third bass). These words provide the basis of a description of a "magical oriental night" that incorporates all of them. This second system greatly increases the number of possible variations. In the old system, variations were limited to the definitions of the same word in a dictionary of common usage, and hence it was possible to discover "the two words that are the inductor couple," *billard* and *pillard,* for example (*DL* 42). Now, however, the generating sentence is completely irretrievable. "To discover it too many diverging paths have to be retraced, too many crossroads encountered: it has been pulverized. . . . Roussel himself lost most of the . . . keys, and except by luck this first language cannot be recovered. . . . The forms of dispersion authorized by the sentence such as *'J'ai du bon tabac'* (I've got good tobacco) are infinitely numerous; each syllable offers a new possibility" (*DL* 43).

In an interview published as the postscript to *Death and the Labyrinth* Foucault gives a variety of reasons for his interest in Roussel, which include parallels between some of his books and the novels of Alain Robbe-Grillet and the French literary movement of the *nouveau roman* (new novel). *Death and the Labyrinth* also reveals many thematic grounds for such interest: the preoccupation with death is the most obvious. Furthermore, Foucault denies that his study of Roussel led him to anything else, saying that "I have kept my love of Roussel as something gratuitous" (*DL* 184). Nevertheless, an earlier passage in the interview suggests that the connection between Roussel and Foucault's other interests was there from the beginning:

It is the interest I have in modes of discourse, that is to say, not so much in the linguistic structure . . . but rather the fact that we live in a world in which things have been said. These spoken words in reality are not . . . a wind that passes without leaving a trace, but in fact, diverse as are the traces, they do remain. We live in a world completely marked by, all laced with, discourse, that is to say, utterances which have been spoken, of things said, of affirmations, interrogations, of discourses which have already occurred. To that extent, the historical world in which we live cannot be dissociated from all the elements of discourse which have inhabited this world and continue to live in it as the economic process, the demographic, et cetera, et cetera. . . . In certain of Roussel's works nothing is given at the beginning except the possibility of encountering the "already said," and with this "found language" to construct, according to his rules, a certain number of things, but on the condition that they always refer back to the "already said."
(*DL* 177)

As we will see, the project described in the *Archaeology of Knowledge* would have us treat all discursive systems as if they were based upon "found language" and thus analyzable in terms of the forms of the dispersion that they may yield. In short, *The Archaeology of Knowledge* proposes that we treat all discourse as if it were the product of a Rousselian machine.

The Archaeology of Knowledge

Of all of Foucault's books, *The Archaeology of Knowledge* has produced the most diverse response, both in terms of evaluation and interpretation. Perhaps the most common understanding of the book is articulated by Sheridan who calls it a "theoretical postscript" to *The Order of Things*.[3] Foucault himself describes *The Archaeology of Knowledge* as an attempt to give greater coherence to the enterprise of *Madness and Civilization, The Birth of the Clinic,* and *The Order of Things,* but he also notes that although *The Archaeology* differs on many points and presents some corrections of the earlier books, it could not have been written without them since it relies on results contained in them (*AK* 14–16). But some critics, Racevskis, and Dreyfus and Rabinow, treat *The Archaeology* as if it were at least as important as any of the earlier books, and when they do it seems to be far more than a postscript. Most commentators have treated *The Archaeology* as representative of a method that Foucault would soon improve upon with his move to genealogy, but Cousins and Hussain take the opposite view in calling it "a curiously unexploited text, not least by Foucault himself."[4] Perhaps the strangest treatment of the book is by Alan Megill who argues that it is a parody of method, at least partly on the grounds that Foucault is profoundly antimethodological, and hence could not write a serious work of methodology.[5]

Although there is little support for Megill's view, it is a measure of the strangeness of *The Archaeology of Knowledge* that such a position could be maintained at all. Unlike any other of Foucault's books, *The Archaeology* is characterized by unrelieved abstraction. The occasional examples that do occur are most often references to Foucault's own books and depend upon one's familiarity with them. The abstraction is made all the worse by the fact that enormous numbers of terms are introduced, defined, and then forgotten so that they disappear entirely since they appear nowhere else in Foucault's work. Furthermore, the book seems to consist largely of negative comparisons that explain what Foucault's terms and categories are not, without telling us what they are. Nor is the book methodological in the straightforward sense that one could simply follow it as a set of instructions. In fact, Foucault himself says that the book will be concerned with "theoretical problems" rather than "questions of procedure" (*AK* 21).

Perhaps the easiest way to understand *The Archaeology* is to view it as an attempt by Foucault to specify what distinguishes his work from traditional means of writing history, especially the history of ideas. We might think of "archaeology" as the history of ideas without ideas and without history. That is, Foucault is trying to describe past forms of knowledge without resorting to transcendental entities as guarantors of unity. Traditionally the history of ideas, when it has not treated ideas as unchanging Platonic essences, has invoked other transcendental devices to account for the distinctive character of different bodies of knowledge. The unities of discourse Foucault seeks to be rid of—tradition, influence, development, evolution, spirit, oeuvre—are all ways of conceiving history as continuous. Foucault seeks instead to conceive of the past in terms such as discontinuity, rupture, threshold, limit, series, and transformation. In place of ideas, Foucault seeks to describe statements in "discursive formations," by which Foucault means things like medicine, economics, or grammar understood as "large groups of statements" unified by a "system of dispersion" (*AK* 37). In other words, Foucault is asserting that there is no positive unity to these fields. Statements in any one field lack a common object, style, body of concepts, or group of themes. What unites them, then, is a body of inexplicit "rules of formation" that determine how new statements may be produced within a given formation.

The word *statement* in *The Archaeology of Knowledge* is a translation of *énoncé*, which lacks some of the connotations of the English word that identify it strongly with the content of a linguistic act. The "statement" has been a major concern, for example, of philosophers in the analytic tradition who have been specifically interested in establishing the conditions of truth claims. But Foucault is not interested in either the truth claims or any other feature of the content of statements. Rather, his *énoncé* is defined purely in terms of its function within a discursive formation. An *énoncé* is not a part of everyday speech, but, as Dreyfus and Rabinow describe it, "a serious speech act" intended to be part of a body of knowledge. The archaeologist's task is to subject each *énoncé* to a double reduction:

"Not only must the investigator bracket the *truth* claims of the serious speech acts he is investigating—Husserl's phenomenological reduction—he must also bracket the *meaning* claims of the speech acts he studies; that is, he not only must remain neutral as to whether what a statement asserts as true is in fact true, he must remain neutral as to whether each specific truth claim even makes sense. . . ."[6]

Discursive formations are made up of serious speech acts that Foucault refuses to take seriously, but rather treats as if they were geometries or symbolic logics. Each *énoncé* is understood as part of something like a closed system entirely independent of any larger context. "This decontextualizing which does away with the horizon of intelligibility and meaning . . . leaves only a logical space for possible permutations of types of statements."[7] Thus Foucault treats discursive formations as if they were like Roussel's novels, consisting of permutations of an originating set of *énoncés*. Such permutations are limited by the rules of formation proper to the particular discursive formation, just as Roussel's different novels were generated by different rules of transformation. Another analogy to Foucault's method is transformational grammar, which holds that certain rules of transformation permit a sentence to be restated in a variety of syntactical structures. In each case the operation is more or less mechanical, requiring no consciousness to found truth or meaning. This is what Foucault means when he says that he has defined "a method of analysis purged of all anthropologism" (*AK* 16).

Dispersion is the term that describes both the workings of Roussel's novel-making machines and the workings of fields of knowledge under archaeological analysis. A discursive formation is defined by the relationship of its dispersed parts, its objects, concepts, types of statement, and thematic choices, in regular patterns of order, correlation, position, function, or transformation. As the word dispersion suggests, a discursive formation is thus characterized by a kind of structured randomness, much like the order that a liquid has in forming a pattern of droplets as it spills, or that seeds will have as they are cast over the earth. This is doubtless a bizarre way to think about divisions of knowledge, and Foucault explicitly rejects most of the terms that derive from the usual methods: science, ideology, theory, or domain of objectivity. Now there are as many ways of conceiving of knowledge as there are terms such as these, but there are two conceptions that have been most important. One of them, positivism, treats a field of knowledge as structured by the rationality appropriate to its subject matter. Thus in this view, the form of biology is a result of the natural forms of life to which the truth of biology corresponds. The other position, which is perhaps best articulated by Frankfurt School philosophers, especially Mannheim and Habermas, holds that knowledge is constructed in response to the interests of a particular group or class. In this view, the structure of knowledge is largely determined by its social, political, or institutional context. Foucault's archaeology rejects both of these positions by treating fields of knowledge as if they were independent of both real objects and interested subjects.

Foucault's earlier work never articulates such an extreme position. In fact, it is quite clear that the interests of those in power play some role in the changing definitions of madness, and the shift in the medical gaze. But we can also see how *The Archaeology* does account for much in both *The Birth of the Clinic* and *The Order of Things.* In both cases we observed the disorienting tendency of Foucault to withhold judgment when he presents historical systems of thought, so that we find ourselves in the midst of the Renaissance *episteme,* for example, without the usual guideposts telling us either that what was believed then is considered false now or that allowing for superficial differences it was really the same as what we believe now. I noted the play among the three points on the triangle in *The Birth of the Clinic,* and the even more complex permutations of the quadrilateral of language in *The Order of Things.* In each case, within a given historical field the character of knowledge and the transformations it is capable of are defined by the relations of a set of terms and the rules by which the particular discursive formation is produced from the original or structuring set. Thus natural history is a product of the relations among attribution, articulation, derivation, and designation as applied to living beings; when the relations among the four terms are altered, the same application produces biology. To say that biology or natural history are produced is to say that their concepts, objects, themes, and statements are all derived from the epistemic structure, and that they cannot exist outside of the particular discursive formation.

This method of investigating knowledge or discourse is likely to allow us to see things that the history of ideas or history of science will now allow. Those studies have characteristically ignored any sense in which a branch of knowledge might be self-generating, and have tended to discuss the self-limiting characteristics of historical disciplines only in terms of the errors they espoused. Archaeology shows us what is proper to a historical field and thereby keeps us from anachronistic interpretations of it. It also strongly suggests the inadequacy of understanding the formation of knowledge in terms only of objects or interests by showing that a field's own internal character as a dispersion of *énoncés* can explain why there can be a feature of that field that neither corresponds to reality nor serves the interests of the powerful. Nevertheless, archaeology is an inadequate method when used in isolation, and Foucault himself began to realize this fact soon after he completed *The Archaeology*. What Foucault's new method, genealogy, will take into account are the power relations in which every discursive formation must be situated. Before we take up genealogy, however, we need to look at elements of *The Archaeology of Knowledge* and the related influential essay, "The Discourse on Language," that already reflect some of the principles of the later method.

The Control of Discourse

Chapter 4 of *The Archaeology of Knowledge* deals with the formation of "enunciative modalities," which might be defined as the conditions under which an *énoncé* might be uttered. The questions that define the modalities are: who is speaking, from what institutional site is he speaking, and what is his relationship to the objects of his discourse. "Who is speaking" asks from what position in the hierarchy of those who might utter this particular discourse is it actually being uttered. For example, "Medical statements cannot come from anybody; their value, efficacy, even their therapeutic powers, and, generally speaking, their existence as medical statements cannot be dissociated from the statutorily defined person who has the right to make them" (*AK* 51). The same sentence uttered by a carpenter and a doctor would not be the same *énoncé* within the field of medicine. Similarly, an *énoncé* will be affected by its institutional site, which might be a university, a hospital, a laboratory, or a government bureau, but also a documentary site such as a book, a case history, or another kind of record. The modality of an *énoncé* will also be affected by a speaker's relation to the objects of a discursive formation; he may be a listener, a questioner, an observer, etc., and each will qualify the *énoncé* in a particular way.

Thus the natural historian is related to living beings as a pure observer since all characteristics on the table were visual, but the biologist was not merely an observer; he was more importantly one who used instruments to dissect and uncover what was invisible.

These modalities are not strictly internal to the system of statements, but apparently are not external to it either in the sense that real objects or subjects are held to be. All of the questions seem to pertain to a subject, and therefore Foucault might seem to be guilty of the anthropologism he has sworn to avoid. But, in fact, Foucault is not inquiring about actual subjects here, but about "subject positions" that are more or less defined by the discourse itself. Thus the subject does not have the unifying function, which, as man, he has held since the beginning of the nineteenth century. The enunciative modalities, rather, manifest the subject's dispersion "to the various statuses, the various sites, the various positions that he can occupy or be given when making a discourse" (*AK* 54). What holds these modalities together within a field is not the activity of a prediscursive consciousness, but "the specificity of a discursive practice. . . . Thus conceived, discourse is not the majestically unfolding manifestation of a thinking, knowing, speaking subject, but, on the contrary, a totality, in which the dispersion of the subject and his discontinuity with himself may be determined" (*AK* 55). Discourse is no longer to be understood as the expression of the speaker, but rather the speaker is to be understood as part of a system of discursive practice.

The dispersion of the subject bears some relation to the "decentering" of the self or subject that has been associated with poststructuralism in general and with Jacques Lacan in particular. Foucault's dispersion might be conceived as a look at the subject from the other side. Lacan attributed to Freud the revolutionary insight that the subject's reality exists not in a conscious, unified self, but in the unconscious that owes its existence not to the self but to others: parents, siblings, etc. The Freudian subject is thus a divided subject. Lacan adds that the unconscious is the *discourse* of the Other, that it is a product of language. The unconscious constitutes the subject but is inaccessible to him; he is thus not only divided among ego, super-ego, and id, but also by being unable to capture his being, which is the Other's discourse and not his own. Foucault looks at this process not from the point of view of the self, but from that of discourse. That the subject is dispersed within a discursive formation says nothing about what it might feel like to experience that formation; rather, it tells us something about the authority or the foundation that discourse carries. Such authority or foundation cannot be found in the *cogito*, the transcendental subject, but only within the positions defined by the discursive practice itself.

The notion of subject position is important in Foucault's own intellectual development. While the examples that he gives show that he was thinking of the question of enunciative modalities as early as *The Birth of the Clinic*, Foucault in *The Archaeology* for the first time becomes explicit about the issue of power. Thus the status of the speaker becomes first a question of modality, where it had received scant notice earlier. A dispute over the control of a discourse is noted between the university faculties and the Royal Society over medicine in late eighteenth-century France, but the role of these kinds of institutions remains untheorized in *The Birth of the Clinic*. In *The Archaeology*, and even more importantly in "The Discourse on Language," discursive practices are increasingly seen as limiting and exclusionary. In taking up this theme, Foucault moves definitively beyond the structuralism that would define discourse solely as a matter of the relations of key terms and the possible statements that may be derived from them. That kind of structure is now seen as part of a larger practice that is not merely linguistic or intellectual, but social.

It is not clear exactly when Foucault theoretically formulated a position—genealogy—that would no longer treat discursive practices as radically isolated from nondiscursive, social contexts, but "The Discourse on Language" already does this practically. The change is in part a result of that piece having first been given as Foucault's inaugural lecture at the Collège de France. Foucault begins by saying that it is hard to begin, that he would rather have been perceived as a nameless voice, as if he wished he were merely the effect of discourse that *The Archaeology* would describe him as. But the reality of his institutional standing seems to prohibit that, for it is institutions rather than discourse that dominate "The Discourse on Language." In response to his fear of beginning, Foucault imagines institutions replying: " 'But you have nothing to fear from launching out; we're here to show you discourse is within the established order of things . . . that a place has been set aside for it—a place which both honors and disarms it; and if it should happen to have a certain power, then it is we, and we alone, who give it that power' " (DC 216). Foucault states his hypothesis in this lecture as having to do not with discourse as a self-contained system, but about its social control: "I am supposing that in every society the production of discourse is at once controlled, selected, organized and redistributed according to a certain number of procedures, whose role is to avert its powers and its dangers, to cope with chance events, to evade its ponderous, awesome materiality" (DC 216). It is almost as if Foucault now holds that discourse could live the isolated, self-reproducing existence Foucault described for it, but society fears allowing discourse this freedom, and so interferes.

"The Discourse on Language" first takes up "rules of exclusion," which are various ways by which discourse can be denied. These include simple prohibition: "We know perfectly well that we are not free to say just anything, that we cannot simply speak of anything, when we like or where we like. . . . the areas where . . . the danger spots are most numerous are those dealing with politics and sexuality" (DC 216). Some discourse is not prohibited, but merely rejected. Thus the speech of the mad was not really listened to by doctors before the eighteenth century even though what the mad said defined the difference between reason and madness. Finally, the division between the true and the false excludes much discourse, and it does so just as the other forms of exclusion do: by means of institutional support including schools, publishers, libraries, learned societies, etc. Foucault's point is that it is the power of institutions and not the truth of discourse that excludes its false competitors. Notice that these rules of exclusion are similar to the discursive modalities discussed in The Archaeology, but they are located not within discursive practices but within the social practice we call institutions. Foucault now explicitly says these practices are external and that they "concern that part of discourse which deals with power and desire" (DC 220).

Foucault next takes up rules of order, classification, and commentary that deal with another aspect of discourse, that of chance. Here Foucault discusses the same territory that occupied him in The Archaeology, but the emphasis has shifted from production in the earlier work to limitation in this one. Two of these internal limitations we have already had occasion to observe, commentary and the author. What Foucault has to say about each of them here is that they are not stable entities. The difference between what is an "original" text—be it scripture, law, or literature—and a commentary on it changes both in the case of particular texts and in theories that purport to fix such differences. Similarly, we have already noted that the role of authorship does not stay the same even within such areas as science or literature. The third internal limitation that Foucault mentions is that of the disciplines. This is a new category in Foucault's work, one which he previously eschewed: "archaeology does not describe disciplines" (*AK* 178). Now, the word *discipline* seems to mean all that "discursive formation" previously stood for:

. . . disciplines are defined by groups of objects, methods, their corpus of propositions considered to be true, the interplay of rules and definitions, of techniques and tools; all these constitute a sort of anonymous system, freely available to anyone who wishes . . . without there being any question of their meaning or their validity being derived from whoever happened to invent them. . . . In a discipline . . . what is supposed at the point of departure is . . . that which is required for the construction of new statements. For a discipline to exist, there must be the possibility of formulating—and of doing so ad infinitum—fresh propositions." (*DC* 222–23).

So far, a discipline sounds not like a principle of limitation, but of generation. But a discipline is capable of production only within "a narrow framework" (*DC* 222). Foucault's emphasis here is on what a discipline excludes: "A discipline is not the sum total of all the truths that may be uttered concerning something. . . . There are two reasons for this, the first being that . . . disciplines consist of errors as well as truths, errors that are in no way residuals, or foreign bodies, but hav[e] their own positive functions and their own valid history, such that their roles are often indissociable from that of the truths. The other reason is that for a proposition to belong to [a discipline] it must fulfill certain conditions, in a stricter and more complex sense than . . . simple truth" (*DC* 223). A discipline defines its own realm of "truth," which excludes everything that does not fit. Foucault borrows a phrase from his teacher, Canguilhem, that describes the condition a proposition must attain before it can be seriously considered and judged: it must be "within the true" (*DC* 224). Thus Mendel, now regarded as the originator of modern genetics and with Darwin one of the two founders of contemporary biology, had his statements about genetics rejected

by nineteenth-century biology. This rejection has been treated as
something of a mystery by historians of biology, but Foucault argues
that Mendel spoke of objects and employed methods that were not
part of the biology of his era. His theory of genetics was thus not
"within the true" and could not receive a serious hearing.

The limiting power of discipline described in "The Discourse on
Language" is consistent with archaeology in the sense that what
prevents Mendel's genetics from being accepted is entirely internal
to the discourse of biology. But internal constraints now make up
only one of three groups of rules that control discourse. The third
group determines the conditions under which a discourse may be
used, and thus consists of rules that restrict those who may speak
or write it, and that totally deny access to others: "none may enter
into discourse on a specific subject unless he has satisfied certain
conditions or if he is not, from the outset, qualified to do so. More
exactly, not all areas of discourse are equally open and penetrable;
some are forbidden territory (differentiated and differentiating) while
others are virtually open to the winds and stand, without any prior
restrictions, open to all" (DC 224–25). Foucault sees himself as
challenging here "one of the great myths of European culture . . .
the universal communication of knowledge and the infinitely free
exchange of discourse. This notion does not, in fact, stand up to
close examination. Exchange and communication are positive forces
at play within complex but restrictive systems; it is probable that
they cannot operate independently of these" (DC 225). These restrictive systems are rules by which discourse is subjected—that is,
made to serve the interests of those in power—rather than being
freely available to all who might seek the truth.

Among these restrictive systems Foucault includes rituals, which
specify behavior, signs, gestures, etc. that must accompany discourse. The discourses of religion, law, therapy, and politics all are
hard to distinguish from rituals that define the roles of speakers and
listeners. The discourse of psychotherapy, for example, cannot attain
its efficacy except within the ritual setting of the session between
doctor and patient. Fellowships of discourse restrict the use of a
certain discourse to those included within a community or group
of affiliated individuals. Doctrine restricts who may speak a discourse
by causing an individual who adheres to it to be barred from other
discourses. Social appropriation also counts as a system of restriction;
privileged classes are able to learn certain privileged discourses easily,

while these discourses are difficult for others to learn. Most of the time, these systems of restriction work together "constituting great edifices that distribute speakers among different types of discourse, and which appropriate those types of discourse to certain categories of subject" (*DC* 227). Thus, for example, educational systems involve all of the systems by which discourse is subjected, for they inculcate rituals, certify qualification of speakers, constitute groups of doctrinal adherents, and distribute access to discourse.

"The Discourse on Language," then, represents a significant break with the extreme methodological position articulated in *The Archaeology of Knowledge* by no longer treating discourse as a completely self-contained and self-generating machine. Now Foucault places discourse in the context of rules of exclusion and restrictions deriving from social interests and practices. But "The Discourse on Language" remains fundamentally similar to *The Archaeology* in one significant respect: its focus is on discourse. Thus, while Foucault outlines some of the projects he will take up in the future, his description of them reflects an orientation that he will largely have abandoned by the time he actually completes them. For example, he describes a project that would "measure the effect of a discourse claiming to be scientific . . . on the ensemble of practices and prescriptive discourse of which the penal code consists" (*DC* 232). We recognize *Discipline and Punish* as the book that this project became, but its focus is not on science, or discourse, or the penal code per se, but on strategies and techniques of control, the body, and the architecture of prisons. Similarly, the methodological demands—reversal, discontinuity, specificity, exteriority—his projected projects imply, as we saw earlier, apply very well to Foucault's work as a whole, but they are more apparent in the work done prior to "The Discourse on Language" than after. We might say, then, that this lecture represents, if not a rupture in Foucault's oeuvre, at least a picture of it in transformation.

Genealogy

In a body of work as original and difficult as Foucault's, it is hard to identify landmarks that allow that body to be charted, its growth measured and described, its changes noted. Given this situation, which would certainly please Foucault himself, it was probably inevitable that commentators would make much of the shift from archaeology to genealogy. Nevertheless, virtually every commentator also warns against making too much of the change. As Dreyfus and Rabinow put it, in italics: *"There is no pre- and post-archaeology or genealogy in Foucault."*[8] Rather, the change I am discussing here is a matter of whether discourse, or its external limits and conditions, will receive more emphasis, and of the reconceptualization of those limits and conditions. The importance of genealogy is not, then, that we have caught Foucault in a contradiction or that his earlier work should be dismissed because it makes use of a method Foucault ultimately rejected. Foucault never rejected archaeology, except perhaps in the extreme form in which it is described in *The Archaeology of Knowledge*. Genealogy is important because of what it adds to Foucault's repertoire of analytic tools. It is a powerful conception of the relations of history, power, and knowledge.

Foucault mentions genealogy in "The Discourse on Language," but the concept itself is not developed there even if, as we have seen, a genealogical perspective does silently inform much of the lecture. In an essay from the same period, "Nietzsche, Genealogy, History," Foucault does give his first extended treatment of the concept. The word itself comes from Neitzsche's *The Genealogy of Morals,* but Foucault's essay concerns his relationship with Nietzsche's work in general. Several of the points made in this essay indicate genealogy's continuity in Foucault's earlier work. That genealogy "requires patience and a knowledge of details," that it "depends on a vast accumulation of source material," that it constructs " 'monuments' . . . from 'discreet and apparently insignificant truths,' " that it "demands relentless erudition" all confirms that in one sense Foucault always was a genealogist (*NGH* 140).[9] This description also tells us that genealogy opposes itself not to historical research, but to the philosophical conceptions of history that dominated in the nineteenth century and are reflected in Hegel and Marx among others. This "historian's history finds its support outside of time and pretends to base its judgments on apocalyptic objectivity" (*NGH* 152). The kind of history genealogy advocates is " 'effective' history [which] differs from traditional history in being without constants. Nothing in man—not even his body—is sufficiently stable to serve as the basis for self-recognition or for understanding other men" (*NGH* 153). The past can no longer be treated as continuous development, and we must guard against recognizing ourselves there.

Here again, these elements of genealogy have long figured in Foucault's work. *Madness and Civilization,* for example, refuses to allow us to recognize the madness of the past by any modern name or classification, and it refuses to link different historical constructions of "madness" by progress or any other form of continuity.

The second point of consistency is the critique of origins, which Foucault has always taken into account—nowhere in his work do we find the search for origins—and which also played a major role in the discussion of man in *The Order of Things.* "Nietzsche, Genealogy, History" explains why the search for origins must be avoided: "because it is an attempt to capture the exact essence of things . . . because this search assumes the existence of immobile forms that precede the external world of accident and succession" (*NGH* 142). As I have already noted, Foucault's work since *Madness and Civilization* has been characterized by a refusal of essences. It is this refusal that treats madness, illness, and man as historical constructions rather than as fundamental truths. What the genealogist opposes to origins is dispersion: "What is found at the historical beginning of things is not the inviolable identity of their origin; it is the dissension of other things. It is disparity" (*NGH* 142). Thus Foucault's explicit introduction of the term *genealogy* to define his own work is not a repudiation of his early studies of institutions and knowledges, but represents an explanation of the approach they took.

One confusion that readers unfamiliar with Nietzsche may find in the term *genealogy* is its association with family history and biology. Genealogies can be family trees of an individual or of the evolution of a species. Nietzsche borrowed the term from the biological sphere in order to describe morals as having an historical "descent" rather than being "immobile forms" existing from the beginning of time. But Foucault warns that "genealogy does not resemble the evolution of a species and does not map the destiny of a people. On the contrary, to follow the complex course of descent is to maintain passing events in their proper dispersion; it is to identify the accidents, the minute deviations—or conversely, the complete reversals—the errors, the false appraisals, and the faulty calculations that gave birth to those things that continue to exist and have value for us" (*NGH* 146). In other words, accidents determine our knowledge and our condition. Foucault is clearly correct to distinguish this conception of descent from that which would predict the destiny of a people based on their common descent from a group of ancestors, for that is a form of essentialist thinking, the people's identity being fixed forever by its origin. On the other hand, modern biology regards evolution as precisely the product of accidents: random variation, environmental change, structural limitation. It is true that we tend to understand the evolution of a species from the point of view of those that survive today, and thus treat their survival as if it were somehow necessary rather than accidental. But as Stephen J. Gould has argued, we cannot account for the current forms of species by assuming that all of their features developed *because* they served an adaptive advantage, and we misunderstand evolutionary history if we regard those species currently existing as better or more advanced than earlier species, which may have survived many millions of years longer. Instead of depicting evolutionary history as a ladder of development, Gould suggests that it be pictured as a bush, and in this conception current species turn out to be mere twigs. Thus in discussing the evolution of the horse, Gould argues

Evolutionary genealogies are copiously branching bushes—and the history of horses is more lush and labyrinthine than most. To be sure, *Hyracotherium* is the base of the trunk (as now known), and *Equus* [the modern horse] is the surviving twig. We can, therefore, draw a pathway of connection from a common beginning to a lone result. But the lineage of modern horses is a twisted and tortuous excursion from one branch to another. . . . Most importantly, the path proceeds not by continuous transformation but by lateral stepping (with geological suddenness . . .). Each lateral step to a new species follows one path among several alternatives. Each extended lineage is a set of decisions at branching points—only one among many hundreds of potential routes through the labyrinth of the bush. There is no central direction, no preferred exit to this maze—just a series of indirect pathways to every twig that ever graced the periphery of the bush.[10]

If evolutionary descent is understood in this way, then Foucault's use of *genealogy* is an accurate, though metaphorical, borrowing. What Gould pictures as a bush, Foucault describes as dispersion. In fact, Gould's genealogy is much closer to Foucault's than is Nietzsche's own *Genealogy of Morals* where Christian morality is traced back to a distinct, if accidental, origin in Judaism seen as the triumph of a "slave revolt in morality."[11] As Foucault implies, Nietzsche was not always a genealogist himself.

What "Nietzsche, Genealogy, History" adds to the concept of descent that is implied in Foucault's earlier work is the role of the body: "descent attaches itself to the body. It inscribes itself in the nervous system, in temperament, in the digestive apparatus; it appears in faulty respiration, in improper diets, in the debilitated and prostrate body of those whose ancestors committed errors" (*NGH* 147). The body will become in *Discipline and Punish* the locus of power relations and the object of disciplinary technology. Prior to this, the body had held a place of some importance in *Madness and Civilization* and *The Birth of the Clinic*, but descent in these books is mainly traced through discourse and through the gaze. Now, discourse and the gaze become means by which the body is inscribed and dominated. Foucault does not mean the body to be understood as a biological entity that is constructed literally from genetic materials or defined by instinctual forces. Rather, he treats the body almost as pragmatists such as William James and John Dewey treated the mind: as the repository of habits. The difference is that the pragmatists regarded habits as in principle capable of modification or self-conscious creation, no matter how powerful their ingraining might be. Foucault's conception of the body has it inscribed by forces largely beyond the control of the individual because they are a function of history. The task of genealogy "is to expose a body totally imprinted by history and the process of history's destruction of the body" (*NGH* 148).

The most important change signaled by Foucault's new emphasis on genealogy, however, is the conception of history as "a single drama . . . the endlessly repeated play of dominations" (*NGH* 150). Here Foucault remains very close to Nietzsche whose genealogy of Western morality asserts that the good is etymologically identified with the noble, the aristocratic, the dominant, and the bad with the low, the common, and the unhappy.[12] The triumph of good over bad is never a matter of simple virtue, or selflessness or peace, but of the violent imposition of law. Domination is not a relationship; it cannot be imagined in terms of the interaction of two free and consenting subjects capable of reconciling their differences. Rather, domination "is fixed, throughout its history, in rituals, in meticulous procedures that impose rights and obligations. It establishes marks of its power and engraves memories on things and even within bodies. It . . . gives rise to the universe of rules, which is by no means designed to temper violence, but rather to satisfy it" (*NGH* 150).

The accidents of history are no longer seen as the product of the mere recombination of the elements of the deep structure of discourse. History is still conceived as a succession of systems governed by rules, but these systems are now called regimes, and the rules are "empty in themselves, violent and unfinalized; they are impersonal and can be bent to any purpose. The successes of history belong to those who are capable of seizing these rules" (*NGH* 151). Interpretation takes on a new meaning in light of this view of history. It is no longer the attempt to uncover the meaning in an origin, but the appropriation of an arbitrary and meaningless system of rules by those who emerge as dominant in order to impose a new direction upon it or to replace the primary rules with secondary ones. Thus "the development of humanity is a series of interpretations. The role of genealogy is to record its history" (*NGH* 152). Interpretation here is no longer synonymous with commentary, the effort to uncover the buried truth or essential meaning of discourse, but the establishment by a dominant group of its version of the truth. Given this situation, the genealogist can no longer treat history or any knowledge as if it were the product of some omniscient observer, but must understand knowledge as perspective, as an interpretation.

The Archaeology had tried to account for knowledge as the product of autonomous structures that limit in advance what statements a discursive formation can make. Both the production and limitation of statements is treated by archaeology as mechanical rather than rational, as neither meaningful nor explicable in any terms outside of the rules that govern the discursive formation itself. Thus, while archaeology can "survey and order history" in its treatment of successive discursive formations, it does so from an ahistorical perspective, a perspective that denies it is a perspective.[13] In the genealogical position articulated in "Nietzsche, Genealogy, History," knowledge becomes, like morality, a product of the historical play of dominations. Genealogy puts knowledge back into history, and it also puts the genealogist, the historian, the knower there: "according to the mask it bears, historical consciousness is neutral, devoid of passions, and committed solely to truth. But if it examines itself and if, more generally, it interrogates the various forms of scientific consciousness in its history, it finds that all these forms and transformations are aspects of the will to knowledge: instinct, passion, the inquisitor's devotion, cruel subtlety, and malice" (*NGH* 162). The will to knowledge, or will to truth, is "a norm by which power seeks to protect itself by mystifying its control over knowledge."[14] Knowledge is based upon injustice, for there is no right to truth, no foundation for truth. Knowledge under the genealogical perspective regains the meaning and seriousness that it lost under archaeology, but its meaning is not the one it proclaims, but the one it receives from its political and historical position.

The concept of genealogy articulated in "Nietzsche, Genealogy, History" will allow Foucault to return to his critique of institutions and the fields of knowledge that support them in *Discipline and Punish*. The articulation of genealogy also sets the stage for power/ knowledge and bio-power, two notions that Foucault will develop in *Discipline and Punish*, volume 1 of *The History of Sexuality* and in *Power/Knowledge*. Both of these terms reflect the intimacy that humans have with power: it is inextricably intertwined in our bodies and in our truth. Knowledge or truth are no longer for Foucault, as they were for the humanists, the enemies of power, but are absolutely essential to its functioning. In *Discipline and Punish* and in *The History of Sexuality*, Foucault will write fully genealogical histories for the first time. In each discourse takes its place beside techniques, practices, and rituals as a way in which power/knowledge is maintained and extended.

Chapter Six
Disciplinary Technologies and the Constitution of Individuals

Although *The Order of Things* was the book that established Foucault's place among the leading thinkers of our era and continues to be identified by some as his "masterpiece,"[1] there is a strong case to be made for *Discipline and Punish: The Birth of the Prison* as Foucault's most important book, the one that will in the long run have the greatest impact. The book is a synthesis of the themes and approaches that have appeared in earlier works. From *Madness and Civilization* there is the subject of incarceration itself and its economic and political motives. From *The Birth of Clinic* the gaze returns, now in the form of surveillance. Like *The Order of Things, Discipline and Punish* gives an archaeology of a human science, in this instance, penology. Three distinct formations of juridical discourse are treated as strata separated from each other by historical ruptures. But in light of Foucault's more genealogical perspective, they could not be treated as autonomous discourses. On the contrary, each is seen as integrally connected to the larger social and political context of its era. Nor are they treated as purely discursive, but rather as part of an ensemble that includes practices such as torture and examination. What is especially powerful about the argument of *Discipline and Punish* is that the prison is treated as representative of a group of strategies and techniques Foucault calls "discipline" that have characterized power in Western society since the nineteenth century. By making claims that go beyond particular bodies of knowledge and beyond epistemology, *Discipline and Punish* represents Foucault's decision to explicitly take up politics and social theory, areas that his earlier work addressed mainly by implication.

In making broader claims and thus attracting attention from more diverse quarters, *Discipline and Punish* has also offended more people than the other works. Mark Poster observes, for example, that "the methodology of *Discipline and Punish* resounds with dissonance to the ears of Marxists and liberals."[2] The book offends Marxists because discipline is given its own etiology, and is not treated as a mere effect of a mode of production. It offends liberals because it calls into question liberalism's narrative of progress toward an ever freer, more humane social order. Foucault's earlier work also caused offense on these same grounds, but *Discipline and Punish* poses a greater challenge because it offers a coherent analysis of modern social practices that can compete on equal footing with Marxist and liberal accounts. In *Discipline and Punish,* Foucault removes the discussion of power from the context of political theory, but in doing so he offers us a new form of analysis that bears on what we would normally consider political questions.

Torture and Punishment

Foucault begins *Discipline and Punish* with perhaps his most effective opening gambit. Like the description of Pomme's cure in *The Birth of the Clinic* and the account of Borges's taxonomy in *The Order of Things,* the beginning of *Discipline and Punish* is an exercise in defamiliarization. We are meant to experience at once the alterity of another historical reality, and thus to be unable to "recognize" ourselves in it. But also as in the earlier examples, we will come to understand this otherness as having its own logic, its own order.

On 2 March 1757 Damiens the regicide was condemned "to make the *amende honorable* before the main door of the Church of Paris," where he was to be "taken and conveyed in a cart, wearing nothing but a shirt, holding a torch of burning wax weighing two pounds"; then, "in the said cart, to the Place de Grève, where, on a scaffold that will be erected there, the flesh will be torn from his breasts, arms, thighs and calves with red-hot pincers, his right hand, holding the knife with which he committed the said parricide, burnt with sulphur, and, on those places where the flesh will be torn away, poured molten lead, boiling oil, burning resin, wax and sulphur melted together and then his body drawn and quartered by four horses and his limbs and body consumed by fire, reduced to ashes and his ashes thrown to the winds."[3]

Robert François Damiens was to suffer this punishment because he attempted to stab Louis XV. It will be noted that most of the preceding quotation is not in Foucault's own words, but is quoted

from official documents of the time. It describes the torture prescribed for Damiens. Foucault continues for a total of three pages
to quote various accounts of Damiens's torture giving additional
information about the event itself. This material suggests that the
torture may have been even worse than the government had intended. The horses, for example, were unable to successfully quarter
the man even after two more were added to the task; his arms and
legs had to be cut off. Although an executioner pronounced him
dead after the horses finally pulled the limbs away, witnesses reported seeing his jaw move as if he were talking, and another
executioner admitted later that he was still alive when they threw
the torso on the stake. Clearly this account is designed to shock,
but it also serves another purpose: it allows us temporarily to feel
our age superior to earlier ones for having replaced these barbarous,
irrational practices with humane, scientifically informed ones. We
may not have conceived of earlier forms of punishment in quite the
detail Foucault's sources give us, but we are generally convinced
that our methods are better. The story of Damiens's torture makes
us aware of this assumption so that the rest of the book can call it
into question.

Damiens's story is immediately contrasted with the rules for the
house of young prisoners in Paris, drawn up eighty years after the
regicide went to the scaffold. The rules Foucault quotes are a timetable for the prisoners' day. They prescribe no physical pain, no
explicit punishment beyond confinement itself and, perhaps, their
own rigor. The public execution and the timetable "do not punish
the same crimes or the same type of delinquent. But they each define
a certain penal style. Less than a century separates them. It was a
time when, in Europe and in the United States, the entire economy
of punishment was redistributed" (*DP* 7). This period was characterized by various reform projects, and it saw the emergences of a
new theory of law and crime, and a new moral and political justification of punishment. It was during this period, for example, that
the Bill of Rights amended the United States Constitution to prohibit cruel and unusual punishment.

Discipline and Punish as a whole gives an account of a variety of
changes in the punishment of criminals, but it begins by focusing
on the disappearance of public torture. While this seems to be quite
an insignificant change compared to some of the others, Foucault
argues that we may have been too ready to explain it as humani-

zation. The first aspect of the change Foucault calls our attention to is that the abolition of torture coincides with the literal disappearance of punishment. Punishment during the early nineteenth century stops being a spectacle and becomes hidden within the walls of prisons. Second, Foucault notes that the body plays a different role in punishment when physical pain is no longer its object. The body now becomes an intermediary in an economy of suspended rights. It remains affected by punishment, but only as a means of reforming the soul. Capital punishment continued, of course, but its practice became devoid of most elements of torture, the convict being put to death quickly and with as little pain as possible.

The change that Foucault describes here cannot be described as a shift from the irrational to the rational, or from the barbarous to the civilized. Torture as it was practiced from the Middle Ages through the eighteenth century was neither lawless nor primitive. It was prescribed by law, its means and ends clearly understood in advance, its instruments and techniques, as in the case of Damiens, sometimes tending to the baroque. For punishment to be torture it must have three characteristics: it must produce a measured quantity of pain; it must mark the victim; it must be a public spectacle. Torture does not attack the body indiscriminately; the precise degree of pain is predetermined by the number of lashes to be administered, whether the convict is to be allowed to die quickly, what forms of mutilation will be used, etc. Marking the convict is necessary because torture is not meant to purge the crime, but to leave visible signs of punishment on the criminal. Finally, torture is a ritual that requires an audience; its excess of violence is part of a kind of theater, and thus the torture continues even after death when corpses are burnt, mutilated, or displayed. This spectacle is necessary because torture is the expression of the power that punishes.

In addition to this penal torture, juridical torture was also practiced. While penal torture was designed to display the truth of a crime, the aim of juridical torture was to uncover its truth. Such torture figured in a complex and orderly system of criminal investigation and judgment. Unlike modern Western justice that regards guilt and innocence as mutually exclusive, the system that existed prior to the late eighteenth century measured gradations of guilt based upon the degree of evidence available. Evidence of guilt could yield full-proofs, sufficient in themselves to support any punishment; semi-proofs, two of which equal a full proof; and *adminicule* clues, enough of which could be combined to form a semi-proof, although no number of these, however large, could equal a full-proof. The investigation that would yield these proofs was conducted in secret, and it was designed to produce truth in the absence of the accused. Nevertheless, confession was the best of all possible proofs, and juridical torture was meant to produce confessions. This procedure retained much from the medieval trial by ordeal; it was really a contest between the investigator and the accused. If the accused held out in the face of the torture, he was to be presumed innocent. Like penal torture, juridical torture was a regulated practice, "not a way of obtaining the truth at all costs; it was not the unrestrained torture of modern interrogations; it was certainly cruel, but it was not savage" (DP 40). Local codes prescribed the way the procedure should be carried out. There were various degrees of torture, the first of which was the sight of the instruments; children and people over seventy were protected from torture beyond this degree.

There was no strict separation of the means of discovery of truth and the penalty for the crime. Since the accused was already at least slightly guilty because he was suspected of a crime, he was thought to deserve the pain of his interrogation. The ordeal of juridical torture made the body of the accused yield its own truth, even as it began to punish that body. After the final judgment and sentence, the body of the condemned continued to be "an essential element in the ceremonial of public punishment. It was the task of the guilty man to bear openly his condemnation and the truth of the crime that he had committed. His body, displayed, exhibited in procession, tortured, served as the public support of a procedure that had hitherto remained in the shade; in him, on him, the sentence had to be legible for all" (DP 43). Besides displaying the truth of the charge against the condemned, public torture also was the scene of public confession, sometimes of new information divulged by the condemned in order to prolong their lives. Moreover, the tortures connected the punishment to the crime by use of symbols such as Damiens's being made to hold the knife with which he committed the attack. Finally, the suffering of the condemned refers to the eternal punishment that it may either precede or prevent; the drama of the salvation of the soul is played out in the suffering and attitude of the one being executed. Thus the body "has produced and reproduced the truth of the crime. . . . The body, several times tortured, provides the synthesis of the reality of the deeds and the truth of the investigation, of the documents of the case and the statements of the criminal, of the crime and the punishment. It is an essential element, therefore, in a penal liturgy, in which it must serve as the partner of a procedure ordered around the formidable rights of the sovereign, the prosecution and secrecy" (*DP* 47).

Public execution was not only a matter of the triumph of judicial truth; it was also the demonstration of political power. Crime during the classical age was understood as an offense against the person of the sovereign. The law was considered his will and the force of the law an extension of his physical force. In prosecuting a crime, the sovereign is replying to one who has offended him, and some portion of the punishment of that person belongs to the sovereign. It is thus never enough that the victim receive redress, for the sovereign must also be satisfied. Revenge is entailed by the fact that power is vested in the sovereign's person. His right to punish is an extension of his right to make war on his enemies. Public execution is a ritual in which the momentarily injured sovereign is restored to his sovereignty. Like a coronation or the entry of the king into a conquered city, it marks the re-establishment of power. Thus punishment is not intended to convey a sense of proportion, "but of imbalance or excess; in this liturgy of punishment, there must be an emphatic affirmation of power and of its intrinsic superiority . . . the physical strength of the sovereign beating down upon the body of his adversary and mastering it" (*DP* 49). The point of the excess of public torture is not mainly one of example, but of terror: "to make everyone aware, through the body of the criminal, of the unrestrained presence of the sovereign. The public execution did not re-establish justice; it reactivated power" (*DP* 49).

Foucault's account of torture in the classical age ascribes it to political needs. Although he admits that in a preindustrial economy labor power and, hence, the human body have less utility and commercial value than in an industrial one and that epidemics and high child mortality rendered death familiar, these factors do not by themselves explain the practice. Rather, "torture was so strongly embedded in legal practice . . . because it revealed the truth and showed the operation of power" (*DP* 55). Power during this era operated as the representation of physical mastery and personal bonds between the sovereign and his subjects. This specific manifestation of power is what produced the penal procedures and spectacles of this period.

Since the public execution was a display of the sovereign's power, it could also be an occasion for his potential weakness to be made manifest. Foucault argues that the people were more than a passive audience at public executions; they were actual participants in the ritual who were expected to perform a service to the king by assisting him in his vengeance. Thus the laws sometimes specifically permitted bystanders to hurl mud and refuse—although not rocks—at criminals in the pillory. But the execution of a criminal could also incite public sympathy for him. In 1775, for example, when participants in the corn riot were executed in Paris, two ranks of soldiers were present, one facing the scaffold, the other facing the people to quell any riot. Here, "the element of spectacle was neutralized" and the public execution ceases to serve its old function; it demonstrates the "political fear" that these ceremonies could arouse (*DP* 65). It would not be lost on French readers that this heavily defended execution took place less than fifteen years before the same regime would be toppled in the French Revolution, which marks for Foucault the beginnings of a new formation of power.

This new formation did not immediately result in the system of incarceration that will become dominant in the nineteenth century. In the late eighteenth century, there are in fact three competing ways of organizing the power to punish. The first of these is the monarchical system of torture, and the third, the modern system of discipline. Foucault calls the second model "punishment." It is dominant in France—and it would appear only in France—from the time of the Revolution until 1810, a mere twenty years. It had been advocated by reformers beginning no earlier than perhaps the middle of the century, and was instituted by the Constituent Assembly in 1791. Many of these reformers were members of the group of intellectuals known as the Idéologues, whose theories of the relations between the individual and society served as the basis for many of the policies of the revolutionary government. But the reforms were also supported by magistrates with royalist sympathies.

The code enacted by the Assembly specified carefully devised penalties designed to fit the crimes they punished. The system used punishment mainly as representation; instead of marking the criminal, it sought to use penalties to dissuade others from committing crimes. The punishment for a crime was devised to represent the evil the wrongdoing had caused. Thus, "he who has used violence in his crime must be subjected to physical pain; he who has been lazy must be sentenced to hard labor; he who has acted despicably will be subjected to infamy" (*DP* 105). This scheme meant that not all punishments the French reformers advocated were free of cruelty; some of them went so far as to suggest that arsonists be burned, and poisoners have poison thrown in their faces prior to execution. In fact, the code prescribed that "every man condemned to death will have his head cut off," but the French reformers' suggestions illustrate the underlying principle of punishment, an analogy between penalty and crime. Analogical punishment is the opposite of torture in that it is not arbitrary; it does not proceed from the whim of a vengeful monarch, but is established in the name of society as a whole consistent with the nature of the crime. "The punishment must proceed from the crime; the law must appear to be a necessity of things, and power must act while concealing itself beneath the gentle force of nature" (*DP* 106).

This representational punishment was thought to work by making the interest in the crime less than the interest in avoiding the penalty. Thus the punishment had to be a lively, intense representation in order to make a greater impression than the advantage the crime might offer. It was to be directed both at prospective criminals and the one being punished in the hope that he will be reformed. For this latter goal to be achieved, punishment cannot be permanent, since it would do no good to make the convict virtuous but imprison him for life. Thus the death penalty is reserved for murderers and traitors, and all other penalties are limited to twenty years. The severity of the penalty itself should diminish as the convict improves; instead of a single painful ordeal, the punishment should consist of a series of progressively less painful privations. In order to affect prospective criminals, punishment must be visible to all. It was suggested that convicts be considered slaves of the state, and be put to work at labor according to the nature of their crimes. Thieves who impede commerce should therefore be put to work rebuilding roads; other public works should be prescribed appropriately for other crimes. In the old system, the condemned became the king's property; under the new system, they became "the property of society, the object of a collective and useful appropriation. . . . Public works meant two things: the collective interest in the punishment of the condemned man and the visible, verifiable character of the punishment. Thus the convict pays twice; by the labor he provides and by the signs that he produces" (*DP* 109). Similarly, public execution must cease to be a festival and a spectacle; instead, it is to be a morality play and a ritual of mourning. Punishment becomes a "recoding" of crime from the terms of private gain to those of public morality. This project would prevent the hero worship of criminals that the system of torture inspired: "if the recoding of punishment is well done, if the ceremony of mourning takes place as it should, the crime can no longer appear as anything but a misfortune, and the criminal as an enemy who must be re-educated into social life" (*DP* 112).

What needs to be emphasized about the notion of punishment as representation is that imprisonment is prescribed only for crimes for which it is appropriate. We tend to forget that prior to the modern era lengthy imprisonment as a penalty was not widely practiced. In the British colonies in North America, for example, jails were used mainly to hold suspects until trial. The first corrective penitentiary in North America was the Walnut Street Prison in Philadelphia, which opened in 1790. Along with earlier experiments in Belgium and England, it was a major influence on penal practices in France which, by the code of 1810, adopted imprisonment as the major form of punishment between fines and death. In several respects the system of punishment as representation seems to have paved the way for the prison. It directed the task of punishment toward the future by seeking to prevent the repetition of crime rather than to expiate it. It also individualized the penalty so that it would suit the character of the particular criminal. Yet Foucault argues that the differences between the two penal systems are far more significant than these similarities. Their most basic difference is the point of application of the penalty. Where representational punishment treated the penalty as a representation and thus directed it in some sense to the criminal's reason, the policy of corrective imprisonment worked on his soul by manipulation. It trained his body to produce correct habits. Why did punishment as representation give way so quickly to another system? One begs the question, according to Foucault, by answering that it was a result of the prestige and influence of American and other foreign examples, since it still remains to be explained why these examples were so appealing. Foucault's answer will be found in his claim that the prison was only one instance of discipline, a developing body of technologies and strategies that come to dominate far more of life than penal practices.

Discipline

But it is not only the visibility and means of punishment that change. Crime itself changes, and this change is not mainly a matter of different acts being committed or new categories of crime being added to the statutes. Rather, crime as it is dealt with by penal practice is no longer merely the matter of determining that an illegal act had been committed and discovering who had committed it. Judgment now determines not only that the act occurred and who did it, but why the act was committed, and it uses this knowledge as a means to determine the appropriate punishment. Thus "a whole set of assessing, diagnostic, prognostic, normative judgments concerning the criminal have become lodged in the framework of penal judgment" (*DP* 19). The French legal code of 1810, for example, treated the determination of madness as absolutely distinct from matters of guilt or punishment. If an act was committed by one who at that time was of unsound mind, the law held that no crime had been committed. But this law was seldom literally observed, and another method for dealing with criminal insanity developed in spite of it. Instead of removing the act from the realm of crime and guilt, madness was used to mitigate guilt and modify punishment. The criminal judged insane was held to be guilty, but in need of treatment rather than punishment, and sentenced to be put away because madness renders him all the more dangerous. But "treatment" is prescribed for more than just insanity; any criminal judgment has become "an assessment of normality and a technical prescription for a possible normalization" (*DP* 21). And the judge is not the only one who makes these judgments; wardens, parole boards and officers, psychiatrists and psychologists, social workers, and others perform their own judgments that affect the actual carrying through of the sentence.

The object of all of these judgments and techniques is the soul, an entity that Foucault regards as quite real, although he does not treat it as a substantial, supernatural being. Rather, the soul is the product of technologies of punishment, supervision, training, and constraint; its reality is historical. "It is the element in which are articulated the effects of a certain type of power and the reference of a certain type of knowledge, the machinery by which the power relations give rise to a possible corpus of knowledge, and knowledge extends and reinforces the effects of this power" (DP 29). The soul is Foucault's name for the field out of which such domains as the psyche, personality, subjectivity, consciousness, etc., have been carved. He uses it to distinguish what he regards as a historical construction of these technologies from what we might be tempted to think is the real man. Rather than freeing that real being from Christian illusion, the modern soul reflects the political mastery of the body: "The soul is the effect and instrument of a political anatomy; the soul is the prison of the body" (DP 30).

It is thus not in the context of crime and punishment that discipline emerges, but in military training. Soldiers, who prior to the late eighteenth century were regarded as being born to their occupation, are afterward *made* by now familiar means. Previously, one found a good soldier by looking for the correct body type. But an ordinance of 1764 describes procedures by which a soldier's body is molded, requiring him to learn a certain posture, to " 'look straight at those [he] pass[es] . . . to remain motionless until the order is given, without moving the head, the hands or the feet . . . lastly to march with a bold step, with knee and ham taut, on the points of the feet, which should face outwards' " (DP 136). The body here is treated not as the subject of the sovereign's power or as a representation of the evils of crime, but as a machine. The disciplinary methods that are used to turn the body into a machine are not entirely new in the eighteenth century. They were to be found earlier "in monasteries, armies, workshops. But in the course of the seventeenth and eighteenth centuries the disciplines became general formulas of domination" (DP 137). Discipline as a general formula of domination borrowed techniques from slavery, servitude, vassalage, and monasticism, but it is distinguished not only by its generality, but also by the fact that it requires and produces aptitude. "Thus discipline produces subjected and practiced, 'docile' bodies. Discipline increases the forces of the body (in economic terms of utility) and diminishes these same forces (in political terms of obedience). . . . disciplinary coercion establishes in the body the constricting link between an increased aptitude and an increased domination" (DP 138). Thus, in treating the body as a machine, discipline uses it more productively than did earlier formations of power, but at a price.

Although the ideas of discipline and the tactics that they produce are specific to militarism, the coercion Foucault is talking about is not perhaps best illustrated by the explicitly coercive and intentionally humiliating methods of military training. The strategies and techniques of discipline that come to pervade Western culture operate more subtly than these. It would therefore be a mistake to take the drill sergeant as the image of the disciplinarian; rather, the foreman, the doctor, or the teacher would be more appropriate. To be sure, the drill sergeant has all of the techniques of discipline at his disposal, but he also relies on such older means as physical bullying and making himself highly visible to his charges. Rather than threats of physical violence that come from a powerful individual, discipline is founded on a meticulous observation of detail combined with an awareness of the political value of those details for purposes of control and efficient use.

Among the most important of these details are those pertaining to the use of space and time. For example, disciplinary strategies enclose space to define it from the rest of the world, and to facilitate maintenance of order and organization. Thus military camps are created and soldiers are no longer billeted in the towns. Factories become large buildings in which an entire process of production can occur and they replace cottage industry. These large spaces are carefully partitioned to give each worker, soldier, or student a proper place, but also to organize more efficiently their work. In classrooms, students come to be positioned by their rank and distributed in an orderly fashion among different sites for learning different lessons. The ordered rows of benches or desks are an empty grid upon which the students are distributed according to their significant differences, and which makes possible both individual instruction and the supervision of all. Time also becomes more rigorously divided into minutes and seconds. Instructions for teachers in some schools were divided into intervals as small as four or five minutes. Timetables come into wide use, and their function is not merely to prevent the waste of time or idleness as had been the case in the monasteries. Now time is ordered to permit its exhaustive use, so that more and more moments may be extracted from time and those moments put to productive use. Thus it is not merely the day which is temporally divided, but bodily actions such as shouldering a rifle or performing an operation in a factory. The more subdivisions that can be assigned to an action, the more that action can be controlled.

The body conceived here is not identical with the conception we normally attribute to the eighteenth century. The Enlightenment is usually known as a period dominated by mechanics, an age in which the body itself was understood as a mechanism. But Foucault argues that a new object was being constituted. Instead of the body as conceived by speculative physics "composed of solids and assigned movements . . . this new object is the natural body, the bearer of forces and the seat of duration; it is the body susceptible to specified operations, which have their order, their stages, their internal conditions, their constituent elements" (DP 155). The body thus appears not merely as one among many wonderful machines the watchmaker God had set in motion, but as an organism with behavior that has its own patterns and requirements. This is not the only one of our beliefs about the Enlightenment that Foucault challenges. This was the period in which Locke and Rousseau gave philosophical expression to a dream of the perfect society based on the contract between the individual and the whole. It is this very ability to consent and contract that we most strongly identify with the political individual as conceived by the Enlightenment. Foucault argues that there was a competing dream, however, this one a military dream of society: "its fundamental reference was . . . not to the primal social contract, but to permanent coercions, not to fundamental rights, but to indefinitely progressive forms of training, not to the general will but to automatic docility" (DP 169).

Foucault should not be understood as saying that this military dream was completely realized anymore than we would argue that Enlightenment principles have produced a utopia. But he is arguing that we need to understand that both dreams express conceptions that help define our world. We know that the philosophical principles of the Enlightenment were transmitted in the form of major documents like the United States Constitution or the Declaration of Independence. The dream of a military society did not triumph at this level of explicit doctrine. Rather than persuading us rationally, it surreptitiously found its way into virtually every aspect of our lives. It came in the form of methods of training, rather than methods of punishing. While we think of military training as enforcing rigid conformity, discipline as Foucault describes it does not turn its subjects into a uniform mass, but distinguishes them by an almost infinite number of means: "Discipline 'makes' individuals; it is the specific technique of a power that regards individuals both as objects and as instruments of its exercise. It is not a triumphant power, which because of its own excess can pride itself on its omnipotence; it is a modest, suspicious power, which functions as a calculated, but permanent economy. . . . The success of disciplinary power derives no doubt from the use of simple instruments; hierarchical observation, normalizing judgment and their combination in a procedure that is specific to it, the examination" (*DP* 170). These three instruments of training produce not only able bodies, but also meticulously differentiated individuals.

Disciplinary observation, or surveillance, is hierarchical both literally and metaphorically. Once again this observation is not the usual observation of Enlightenment science that seeks facts by direct sense experience. It is rather a coercive observation that attains its ends by making the one subjected to it always aware that her actions may be seen. The military camp is an instance of hierarchical observation as metaphor, since such observation is achieved on a flat surface by means of a chain of command in which each higher level observes the one below. But the literal elevation of an observer allows him to keep all of those he supervises under surveillance. Thus in a factory or the dining hall of a school, a platform would be raised to allow the foremen or inspectors to observe all of the workers or students. The demand for observation posed a new problem for architecture: to design buildings not merely to be seen or to permit one to see outside, but to achieve control over individuals on the inside by making all of them visible. Thus the design for a military academy stipulated that pupil's rooms be distributed along a corridor with officer's quarters situated so that every ten pupils had an officer on each side. The pupil's cells had windows on the corridor from chest height to near the ceiling for "disciplinary reasons." Even the latrines were designed to permit observation: they were installed with half-doors so that the legs and head would be visible.

Foucault argues, however, that the hierarchical network or pyramid proved to be a more efficient means of observation even than circular designs—which anticipate Bentham's panopticon prison—permitting constant surveillance from a single point. As factories grew in size, the role of supervisory personnel grew larger and more complicated. These supervisors were no longer masters instructing apprentices, but clerks and foremen who were not themselves workers. Work was regulated by the clock and the workers were believed to need strict, harsh treatment. The guild system, in which a group of workers performing the same crafts regulated themselves, did not fit with capitalism: industrial production, private ownership, and profit all demanded that the agents of the owner continuously supervise the workers. Foucault quotes Marx who in *Capital* argues that "The work of directing, superintending and adjusting becomes one of the functions of capital, from the moment that the labor under the control of capital, becomes cooperative. Once a function of capital, it requires special characteristics" (*DP* 175).

The function of surveillance is not merely negative; it does more than prevent infractions from being committed. It also allows for judgment, evaluation, and ranking that create distinctions and individualize those being observed. Foucault argues that the essential distinction made by a disciplinary regime—an organization where discipline is the predominant technique of control—is between the normal and the abnormal. Normalizing judgment is as constant as surveillance. Disciplinary systems contain their own juridical and penal apparatuses that pertain to a set of rules and offenses against them that did not exist in previous systems. A series of micropenalties are enforced in the factory, the school, and the army for absences and lateness, inattention and lack of zeal, impoliteness or disobedience, etc. "It was a question both of making the slightest departures from correct behavior subject to punishment, and of giving a punitive function to the apparently indifferent elements of the disciplinary apparatus: so that, if necessary, everything might serve to punish the slightest thing; each subject find himself caught in a punishable, punishing universality" (*DP* 178).

But discipline does not control merely by means of punishment and its threat. It also rewards by means of awards. Since disciplinary judgment always measures the subject against a norm or average, it continually creates ranks. Those who are judged to be significantly better than the norm are rewarded by the judgment itself. Typically the system of ranks is more elaborate than the judgment of better or worse than the norm would suggest. Rather, the norm is the basis of a scale, such as the percentile scale on a modern standardized test, which is used to classify and not merely numerically rank. Foucault gives the example of a military academy where slight differences in the uniform made visible a pupil's "honorary" classification. Different colored epaulets distinguished classes ranging from very good, through mediocre, to bad, but the bottom class, the shameful, were forced to wear sackcloth. The privilege of high rank here was the right to be punished in the same way as soldiers were punished: by arrest and imprisonment. These punishments were also applied to lower classifications, but the pupils in these could also be subjected to more humiliating punishments. Thus rank here was its own reward; it allowed one to avoid humiliation but offered no positive benefits except that one was identified as superior. This hierarchy could, of course, be used to place students according to their aptitude and conduct in their postgraduation positions. But it also provided a constant pressure to conform to the same model, and thus attempted to make them all be like one another. "The art of punishing, in the regime of disciplinary power, is aimed neither at expiation, not even precisely at repression. It brings five quite distinct operations into play. . . . The perpetual penalty that traverses all points and supervises every instant in the disciplinary institutions compares, differentiates, hierarchizes, homogenizes, excludes. In short, it *normalizes*" (*DP* 182–83).

Of all the techniques and strategies that discipline has at its disposal none is more characteristic, more widely applied, and more diverse in its forms and manifestations than the examination.

The examination combines the techniques of an observing hierarchy and those of a normalizing judgment. It is a normalizing gaze, a surveillance that makes it possible to qualify, to classify and to punish. It establishes over individuals a visibility through which one differentiates them and judges them. That is why, in all the mechanisms of discipline, the examination is highly ritualized. In it are combined the ceremony of power and the form of the experiment, the deployment of force and the establishment of truth. . . . it manifests the subjection of those who are perceived as objects and the objectification of those who are subjected. (*DP* 184–85)

The examination is at root the gaze of one in power upon one who is less powerful, the subject of that gaze. As we saw in *The Birth of the Clinic*, the medical examination became increasingly important during the classical age, and its character changed as doctors began looking for different things. But *Discipline and Punish* notes that while during the early seventeenth century examinations in hospitals in France were rapid, irregular, and infrequent, by the late eighteenth century doctors had "placed the patient in a situation of almost perpetual examination" (*DP* 186). What interested Foucault about the medical gaze in *The Birth of the Clinic* was the discourse that structured it. What interests him now is that the hospital as organized around the examination, as an "examining apparatus," becomes a site of the production of a different form of knowledge: "the hospital itself, which was once little more than a poorhouse, was to become a place of training and of the correlation of knowledge; it represented a reversal therefore of power relations and the constitution of a corpus of knowledge. The 'well-disciplined' hospital became the physical counterpart of the medical 'discipline' " (*DP* 186). Here Foucault goes beyond his earlier reliance on discourse as the major determinant in the structure of different forms of knowledge, and asserts that the character of medical knowledge was determined by institutional practices that shifted the locus of that knowledge from the books of authorities to the bodies that were offered for examination.

In the schools, tests or examinations, which became the focal point of academic work for students at all levels, are important examples of the same strategy. Although the examined student is not necessarily the subject of a literal gaze, students were asked to regularly display what they had learned, either by speaking or writing answers to questions. Unlike the masterpiece (literally, a work demonstrating mastery of a craft) that a guild member was expected to produce at the end of his apprenticeship to demonstrate his having acquired knowledge, repeated examination provided the teacher with constant knowledge of the pupil. It thus makes possible the beginning of pedagogy as a discipline in its own right.

In his early works Foucault had accounted for new forms of knowledge in terms of changes in the structure of discourse. Now he regards the creation of new fields of knowledge in the modern era as the result of disciplinary techniques and strategies. Several commentators have observed that Foucault is making use of a pun on the word *discipline,* which refers both to a branch of knowledge and to a formation of power. For Michael Walzer this seems to be "nothing more than an elaborate pun" that produces a model of interdependent knowledge and social control that is "too easy."[4] Dreyfus and Rabinow, on the other hand, argue that the pun is "more than simply a rhetorical convergence" because "the very self-definition of the human sciences . . . is closely linked to the spread of disciplinary technologies. . . . The social sciences . . . were first situated within particular institutions of power (hospitals, prisons, administrations) where their role became one of specialization. These institutions needed new, more refined and operationalized discourses and practices."[5] But we can go further than this. Even those branches of knowledge, those disciplines, that we think of as quite ancient, mathematics for example, have developed in the modern era within the university, an institution thoroughly traversed by disciplinary technologies. Not only is the university the place where the regime of truth often comes into contact with the political regime that both supports the university financially and makes use of its knowledge for political ends, but the internal life of the university is also regulated by disciplinary strategies such as academic rank and tenure examinations (or reviews, as they are called). It is true that the content of sciences such as mathematics is less affected by their social organization than is the content of fields such as psychology or literary studies. In these latter fields, the power of examination can eliminate or marginalize individuals and discourses even though these disciplines lack the most minimal theoretical consensus.

The examination represents an explicit instance of the connection between power and knowledge; it linked a particular formation of knowledge to a particular exercise of power. Previously power had always made itself visible; the monarch himself and the symbols that represented him were displayed to establish and maintain his rule, while his subjects remained unseen. As I noted earlier, public torture was one of the ways power was displayed. Under discipline, however, there is an inversion of visibility: the subjects of power become visible, while those who exercise power become invisible. "The examination is the technique by which power, instead of emitting the signs of its potency, instead of imposing a mark on its subjects, holds them in a mechanism of objectification. In this space of domination, disciplinary power manifests its potency, essentially, by arranging objects. The examination is, as it were, the ceremony of this objectification" (*DP* 187).

The knowledge produced by examinations enables for the first time the routine documentation of individuals. Records began to proliferate to accommodate the data generated by examinations. Techniques that are among the most mundane today came into widespread use: registration, file keeping, making of tables and columns. These techniques allowed the individual for the first time to become objectified by description and analysis of his particular development, aptitudes, and abilities. This knowledge could in turn be used for purposes of comparison, or compiled to establish knowledge of groups. Instead of providing knowledge of the essential character of the group, as natural history had provided of species of living beings, disciplinary documentation charted the gaps between individuals in a group or their distribution within a population. As a result of these documentary techniques, each individual became a case. Of course, the lives of some individuals—rulers, heroes, saints—had long been written, but these biographies or hagiographies had served to elevate the individual. The case history turned him into an object and assured his continued subjection. Thus, Foucault argues, discipline marks a reversal of the politics of individualization. Under regimes such as those of feudal Europe, those with the greatest sovereignty were most individualized. The king was more often than anyone else pictured or written about. Under disciplinary regimes, however, power becomes more anonymous and functional. As a result, the least powerful become the most individualized: "the child is more individualized than the adult, the patient more than the healthy man, the madman and the delinquent more than the normal and the non-delinquent" (DP 193). It goes without saying that this form of individuality, produced by hierarchizing surveillance and normalizing judgment, does not carry with it the advantages that individuality conferred when it was associated with power. Thus in recognizing the reality of vast individualization resulting from disciplinary techniques, Foucault is not affirming the Enlightenment conception of society founded by contracts of discrete individuals. He does not deny that the individual is "the fictitious atom of an 'ideological' representation of society; but he is also a reality fabricated by this specific technology of power that [Foucault has] called 'discipline' " (DP 194). Power here no longer is conceived negatively, as repression or censorship for example, but positively as the production of individuals, of knowledge, of domains of objects, of reality itself.

The Prison

So far, I have discussed discipline as a form of training, as a set of technologies of surveillance, and as a means of producing knowledge. I have not yet dealt with it as a replacement for penal torture or for representational punishment in criminal justice and penology. The prison is for Foucault the most characteristic of disciplinary institutions, one which schools, factories, and hospitals all come to resemble. But the prison also appears to be the least successful of disciplinary institutions, where the means of correct training do not seem to work. Characteristically, Foucault will argue that these appearances are deceiving.

The prison, ironic as the thought now seems, began as a utopian project and it inspired a utopian architecture, the most famous example of which is Jeremy Bentham's *Panopticon*. Bentham's design calls for a circular building with an open yard in the middle. In the center of the yard there is a tower with wide windows that make visible the whole of the surrounding building. The cells in this building each have two windows: one on the outside wall allows light into the cell, while one facing the tower makes the inmate visible to the keeper in the tower who cannot in turn be seen by the inmates. The panopticon thus creates the possibility and the illusion of constant surveillance. This architecture is thus the opposite of the dungeon's, which was intended to hide and to deprive of light. The dungeon manifested power by force of thick walls and chains; the panopticon allows power to operate automatically, for even though the guard in the tower may not be looking, the inmate must assume that he is. The panopticon is thus the perfect emblem of discipline, allowing observing power to be completely invisible to the observed subject.

Various panoptic designs for prisons emerged in the nineteenth century, but the prison itself is older. The Rasphus prison of Amsterdam, for example, opened in 1596 and served as a model for eighteenth-century prisons at Ghent in France, Gloucester in England, and for the Walnut Street Prison in Philadelphia. These prisons share the common characteristics of required work, wages for that work, strict supervision, and the use of timetables and other regulations. To these, Gloucester and the Walnut Street Prison in Philadelphia added solitary confinement for some prisoners. What was novel about each of these experiments was that they were designed not merely to punish, but also to reform. Work and reward for that work were meant to teach morality and responsibility. Even solitary confinement was thought to force the prisoner to face his own conscience, meditate on his crime, and resolve to be better.

When the prison emerges in the early nineteenth century as the principal means of punishing criminals, it does mark a significant change in penal practice, but Foucault argues that it did not involve the invention of new techniques: "it was really the opening up of penality to mechanisms of coercion already elaborated elsewhere" (*DP* 231). Although there was resistance at first to a punishment that billed itself as the mere deprivation of liberty, this rationale soon came to seem self-evident. And if Foucault is correct about disciplinary mechanisms having already become pervasive, how could the prison be refused? For if workshops, schools, and hospitals now seem to resemble prisons, these older institutions were in fact models for prisons themselves.

In the strict terms of the law, deprivation of liberty was the only punishment inflicted by a prison. But the whole panoply of micro-penalties came into use in the prison where every aspect of an individual's life could be, and generally was, regulated. Such coercive regulation began with the isolation of the prisoner from society, and, in some of the early prisons, from other prisoners. Isolation was intended to keep the prisoner free from bad influences inside and outside of the prison, and also to bring about moral improvement. But this isolation is another form of individualization which works by eliminating all relationships except those supervised by authority or regulated according to a hierarchy. Foucault asserts this individualization is the primary objective of carceral action. Similarly, prison work is meant to be an agent of carceral transformation, but it cannot be understood in terms of this intention alone; nor can prison work be attributed to an economic motive, even though some unions in the nineteenth century argued that prison work was intended to keep wages low. The motive for penal labor was not profit, "nor even the formation of a useful skill; but the constitution of a power relation, an empty economic form, a schema of individual submission and of adjustment to a production apparatus" (*DP* 243). Penal labor is thus purely disciplinary.

The prison sentence is still often described today as a debt of time the convict owes to society. This suggests that the crime itself has an exchange value equal to a sentence of a certain number of years. But even in the early nineteenth century, the length of a prisoner's actual stay was not determined entirely by his sentence. If the penalty is allowed to become an exchange value, then it loses its effectiveness in bringing about reform. Hence the prison needs a certain degree of independence from the judiciary that allows it to modify sentences in order to successfully transform the inmate. The sentence, then, is like a medical procedure that is continued only so long as it is necessary to help the patient. This analogy suggests the third way in which prisons went beyond the deprivation of liberty: they tried to cure and to normalize. It is the excess beyond the judicial penalty that is the locus of discipline in the prison, that makes it a penitentiary. Before discipline, a criminal was given punishment as retribution for his offense. After discipline, penitentiaries try to make criminals reform, or become normal.

The process of reform required that a knowledge of criminals or offenders be produced. Just as the examination allowed pedagogy to become a science of pupils, the observation of prisoners allowed for the development of a science of criminology, and, offenders, like other subjects of discipline, became cases: "the offender is constituted himself as the object of possible knowledge" (*DP* 251). And yet the object that is constituted is not precisely the "offender," but the "delinquent." An offender is merely someone who has broken a law, committed an offense. The delinquent, on the other hand, is defined not by an act, but by an entire life. Thus biographical knowledge is added to knowledge compiled from direct surveillance of the inmate. The effect of this new way of conceiving of the inmate is to establish "the 'criminal' as existing before the crime and even outside it, and . . . a psychological causality, duplicating the juridical attribution of responsibility. . . . At this point one enters the 'criminological' labyrinth from which we have certainly not yet emerged: any determining cause, because it reduces responsibility, marks the author of the offense with a criminality all the more formidable and demands penitentiary measures that are all the more strict" (*DP* 252). The penitentiary and the delinquent emerge together as products of the same set of strategies and techniques.

To say that discipline produces delinquents is a way of saying that it causes the criminal to be conceived differently, as a type rather than as one who has committed an illegal act. But it is also to say that the penitentiary is responsible for making delinquents of people who previously would have remained mere offenders. Although Foucault is calling into question the objective reality of the criminal personality, the reversal is not really very shocking to us because we are used to hearing the charge that prisons produce criminals. What is surprising is Foucault's discovery that the same charges have been made about prisons since the years when they were first widely introduced. Prisons almost from their beginnings have been accused of breeding criminals and causing crime: they produce delinquents by bringing criminals together to learn from each other and to form a criminal milieu; by making them unfit for life outside; by subjecting freed inmates to conditions that cause them to commit further crimes; and by causing the destitution of the inmate's family. Thus, instead of reforming offenders, prisons have been charged with causing recidivism and with failing to diminish the crime rate.

The response to these charges has been the same throughout the 150 years that they have been made. Either it is asserted that the prisons have been insufficiently corrective because the penitentiary technique remains in need of further development, or that in attempting to be corrective the prison no longer punishes. "The answer to these criticisms was invariably the same: the reintroduction of the invariable principles of penitentiary technique" (DP 268). Foucault isolates seven of these principles that have been reiterated again and again during the history of the prison. They are the same ideas that have already been mentioned here as distinguishing the prison as a disciplinary institution: transformation of behavior, isolation, individualized penalties, work, education, professional supervision, and postrelease surveillance and support. Foucault thus portrays the history of the prison not as a sequence of battles for new reforms, but as the repetition of the battle for the same "reforms," which does not ever fundamentally change the prison, but at most makes it more thoroughly what it has always been.

This leads Foucault to one of his most striking reversals, one the reader is likely to reject out of hand. The prison, even after repeated attempts at reform, consistently fails to reduce crime or reform inmates. But Foucault suggests that this failure is not really a failure at all, and thus that the production of delinquents is the intended consequence of penality. If this were the case,

. . . one would be forced to suppose that the prison, and no doubt punishment in general, is not intended to eliminate offenses, but rather to distinguish them, to distribute them, to use them; that it is not so much that they render docile those who are liable to transgress the law, but that they tend to assimilate the transgression of the laws in a general tactics of subjection. Penality would then appear to be a way of handling

illegalities, of laying down the limits of tolerance, of giving free rein to some, of putting pressure on others, of excluding a particular section, of making another useful, of neutralizing certain individuals and of profiting from others.
(*DP* 272)

The need for this form of control of illegality resulted from the social changes that were marked by the end of the monarchy in France and the general development of industrialization and the market economy. During this period popular illegalities took new forms that posed a threat to those who had gained power as a result of the political revolution and social transformation. Thus illegalities that previously had been limited in their significance—refusal to pay taxes, refusal of conscription, etc.—took on a political dimension during the French Revolution. Furthermore, new illegalities developed that were explicitly political in intent. But the rejection of the laws after the revolution also involved struggles that were not recognized as political in the narrow sense, but were aimed at those whose interests that law served: local land owners, employers, entrepreneurs. Finally, the new regulations enforced by the state, landowners, and employers produced a new class of criminals from people who previously would not have become such; they were pushed outside the law into specialized criminality. New laws to protect bourgeois landed property drove peasants to acts of violence; new laws and regulations also pushed many workers across the boundary between vagabondage and delinquency.

Thus a number of illegal practices seemed to come together to form a new threat. This is not to say that there was an actual political and social movement of illegality, but that such a threat was perceived: "the myth of a barbaric, immoral and outlaw class which . . . haunted the discourse of legislators, philanthropists and investigators into working-class life" (*DP* 275). In the eighteenth century, crime was usually described as resulting from the passions or interests of individuals. But during the early nineteenth century, crime becomes understood as the product of the bottom of the social order. Hence, Foucault argues, the law itself was directed at this class and does not apply equally to all citizens. His point here is not that the laws were unequally enforced, although that may have been true, but that they were created to manage the lower classes, to prevent their illegalities from becoming politically effective or from carrying a social critique. Far from being a failure, then, the prison's longevity is a result of its success in this task of keeping illegality in its apolitical place. Delinquency is the conceptual tool that criminology uses to obtain this end. In this context, even seemingly prosocial analyses, which attribute crime to poverty for example, pathologize the subject, thus rendering his offense the result of a social disease rather than a political inequity. The delinquent is thus made to appear and to feel marginalized while he is being supervised by the prison and the law. The system makes possible the widespread and successful use of delinquents as informers and provocateurs. By this means, but also by "the generalized policing that it authorizes, [delinquency] constitutes a means of perpetual surveillance of the population" (*DP* 281). The prison, while appearing to fail to control crime or reform criminals, succeeds so well at mitigating the political dangers of illegalities that it continues to exist without serious proposals for its abolition.

But the prison is not for Foucault an isolated feature of the social landscape. It is, rather, only the most visible manifestation of the "carceral archipelago," the series of institutions that branch out beyond the frontiers of criminal law (*DP* 297). These institutions are not the schools and the factories that directly train and discipline the majority, but the orphanages, the juvenile reformatories, the rehabilitation centers and halfway houses, the treatment programs and detoxification centers, the asylums in which people may be incarcerated without being convicted of a crime. The penitentiary technique is thus spread throughout the social body. Sin, bad conduct, and crime were once quite separate categories that resulted in penitence, confinement, and court, respectively. Now we deal in subtle gradations in a continuity that runs from the slight departure from the norm to violation of the law. The network of carceral institutions provides a "career path" for delinquents that begins in the orphanage, runs through reform schools and juvenile detention centers, and often leads to prison, the end these other institutions were supposed to prevent. The network by its very ubiquity legitimizes the ever-widening power to punish, which lowers the point at which it is acceptable to be punished. In so doing, the carceral network creates a new kind of law, a law identified with the norm: "The judges of normality are present everywhere. We are in the society of the teacher-judge, the doctor-judge, the educator-judge, the 'social worker'-judge; it is on them that the universal reign of the normative is based; and each individual, wherever he may find himself, subjects to it his body, his gestures, his behavior, his aptitudes, his achievements" (*DP* 304). Thus Foucault concludes, the political issue that the prison raises is not whether we should have something other than the prison. Rather, it is "the steep rise in the use of these mechanisms of normalization and the wide-ranging powers which, through the proliferation of new disciplines, they bring with them" (*DP* 306).

The carceral society Foucault describes is one in which subjects are dominated by a power not their own. But that power cannot be associated with an individual tyrant or with a self-interested ruling class. Rather, at the center of this power structure we find institutions with their architecture, their rules, and their discourses. These institutions do not exclude or repress; they produce, not only material commodities, but the disciplinary individual himself. It is this vision of carceral society that has prompted Foucault's critics to charge him with depicting the social order as a seamless web of power relations.[6] Foucault does give some grounds for this charge. He does not consider the delinquent outside of the law, for example, but entirely inside of it. There is, in his view, no outside. But he does not suggest that disciplinary control is complete or unitary: "ultimately what presides over all of these mechanisms is not the unitary functioning of an apparatus or an institution, but the necessity of combat and the rules of strategy" (*DP* 308). Foucault thus, far from denying the possibility of resistance to this network of power, asserts the inevitability of such resistance.

This conception of power, however, raises another problem, or perhaps the same problem in another register. In volume 1 of *The History of Sexuality*, Foucault devotes a chapter to his conception of power, a conception somewhat revised since *Discipline and Punish*. Resistance is still seen as inevitable, but Foucault has taken the next logical step and now asserts that resistance is produced by power. Although Foucault does not use this metaphor, his description of power does seem to be borrowed loosely from notions of electricity: "Where there is power there is resistance, and yet, or rather consequently, this resistance is never in a position of exteriority in relation to power" (*HS* 95). Resistance, like power itself, is not centered anywhere, but is spread out over the surface of the power network. Since no one holds power, no one can seize it. Foucault here attacks the Marxist conceptions of power centered in a dominant class, of resistance in an oppressed class, and of the possibility of revolutionary change. Here power relations have become a "dense web" and resistance seems not to produce change but the repetition of the same (*HS* 96). One result of this conception of power that Foucault seems to admit is cynicism and pessimism. While Foucault argues that we need to take Machiavelli's cynicism one step further and continue his investigation of the strategies of power now in the absence of the prince, it is not clear what that might produce as a social or political practice. Foucault argues that he favors local struggles, but he is seldom if ever clear about which struggles he would endorse. As will be suggested in the conclusion to this volume, Foucault does not offer us a politics.

In "The Subject and Power" Foucault seems to step back from the extremes of this conception of power when he says that: "if we speak of the structures or the mechanisms of power, it is only insofar as we suppose certain persons exercise power over others" and that "Power is exercised only over free subjects, and only in so far as they are free."[7] As Merquior implies, these pronouncements are dangerously close to the most banal liberalism.[8] They may reflect his shift in focus to the problem of the subject, a change to which his difficulties in conceptualizing power may have contributed. We will see the first step in that change in volume 1 of *The History of Sexuality*.

Chapter Seven
Sexuality and the Will to Knowledge

About halfway through the first volume of *The History of Sexuality*, Foucault asks rhetorically about the aim of the series he was beginning. He answers that it is "to transcribe into history the fable of *Les Bijoux indiscrets*." *Les Bijoux indiscrets*, a novel by the eighteenth-century French writer Diderot, tells of a sultan who receives from a genie a ring that can cause women's sexual organs to speak. The talking sex, Foucault claims, is one of our society's emblems. The value of the sultan's ring was that the sexes it made to speak did not lie; our society, too, has sought, albeit by more prosaic means, to extract the truth of sex. And yet Foucault says that our problem is not only "to know what marvelous ring confers a similar power on us," but also to know "on which master's finger it has been placed; what game of power it makes possible or presupposes, and how it is that each one of us has become a sort of attentive and imprudent sultan with respect to his own sex and that of others. . . . We must write the history of this will to truth" (*HS* 79).

I begin by mentioning an illustration from the middle of the book under discussion here because it is the kind of illustration Foucault typically uses to begin his books. Why does he deviate from his pattern this time? One reason may be that the book as a whole was intended as an introduction to a planned six-volume work. Another might be, however, that Foucault found a more effective opening by narrating the history of sexuality that we most often tell ourselves. In a chapter entitled "We 'Other Victorians,' " Foucault describes the familiar story of the repression of sexuality that begins to develop sometime after the start of the seventeenth century and reaches its full weight during the nineteenth. This repression is the work of a bourgeois morality that restricted sex to the home and to the conjugal family. It imposed silence on sex and established the procreative married couple as the norm for all sexuality. Except for the clandestine world of brothels and pornogra-

phers—those whom Steven Marcus called the "other Victorians"—
modern puritanism has imposed a triple edict of taboo, nonexistence,
and silence. For example, everyone knew "that children had no sex,
which was why they were forbidden to talk about it, why one closed
one's eyes and stopped one's ears whenever they came to show evidence to the contrary, and why a general and studied silence was
imposed" (*HS* 4). Even today, despite Freud, we have escaped this
repression only to a slight degree.

Foucault points out that this narrative about how we have arrived
at our present state of repression coincides with another historical
narrative, the story of the rise of capitalism. The repression, it is
alleged, results from the needs of capitalism for work. Sex distracts
workers from their activities in producing the commodities capitalism needs and is, moreover, especially wasteful if it does not end
in the reproduction of more workers and consumers. But there is
another, hidden reason for this narrative being so often repeated:
"If sex is repressed, that is, condemned to prohibition, nonexistence,
and silence, then the mere fact that one is speaking about it has
the appearance of a deliberate transgression. . . . What sustains
our eagerness to speak of sex in terms of repression is doubtless this
opportunity to speak out against the powers that be, to utter truths
and promise bliss, to link together enlightenment, liberation, and
manifold pleasures; to pronounce a discourse that combines the fervor
of knowledge, the determination to change the laws, and the longing
for the garden of earthly delights" (*HS* 6–7). Thus Foucault suggests
that we have reasons for believing in and repeating this narrative
that have nothing to do with its truth. Our belief that sex is repressed
coincides with our notions of capitalism and acts as an enticement
to speak about sex.

The notion that since the seventeenth century we have lived with
silenced sexuality Foucault calls the "repressive hypothesis." In one
of his most startling reversals, he proceeds to argue not only that
the repressive hypothesis is wrong, but that the period it describes
has experienced an enormous proliferation of discourse about sex.
Far from being silenced, sex has been spoken about more than ever
before. This is not to say that Foucault denies changes in the discourse about sexuality, or that these changes involved some pro-
hibitions. For example, the sexuality of children, which prior to
the seventeenth century could provide an occasion for humor to
people of all social classes, afterward becomes the subject only of

serious discourse. Because the repressive hypothesis entails a certain characterization of power, it provides Foucault with the opportunity to extend the discussion of *Discipline and Punish* in which power is shown to operate in positive as well as negative ways.

The Deployment of Sexuality

To say that sexuality is deployed is already to challenge one of the most tenacious assumptions of modern culture: the identification of sexuality with nature. Certainly this assumption owes much to Freud who treated sex as a drive, the psychological representation of an instinct. Culture was depicted by Freud as demanding the repression of this drive. Like Freud, we tend to identify sex as an element of human nature, and not as something culturally specific. Foucault is obviously not about to deny that there are biological similarities in the human species, among them the sexual form of reproduction. What he is denying, however, is that what we in Europe and North America call sexuality is synonymous with this form of reproduction. Sexuality is both a discourse and a practice that can be shown to have a particular point of emergence in Western culture.

Part of this emergence entails the expanded use of the confession in the Catholic Church. The confession, as an elaborate recollection and description of one's sinful deeds, words, and thoughts, was developed in the monastery both as a spiritual exercise and as a means of control. Monks were taught to master their sinful desires by turning them into discourse. During the Middle Ages, confession was rather infrequent among the general population. Confession manuals from this period, however, prescribe questions that demand explicit answers about the details of sexual acts. By the seventeenth century, however, greater discretion is advised. While this change might seem to support the repressive hypothesis, Foucault notes that this greater discretion is accompanied by an increase in the frequency of confession, in the rigor of self-examination, and in the relative importance of sins of impurity. Thus, instead of restricting itself to describing the details of overt acts, the confession must now include everything that sex might have produced or even merely touched in one's imaginative or mental life. The locus of transgression shifts from one's acts to one's desires, and the whole Church is taught to confess in the manner of monks. Foucault sees a con-

tinuation of this process of turning sex into discourse in the quite
unpenitential writings of the Marquis de Sade and the anonymous
Victorian author of *My Secret Life*. What is important here is not
whether the sex is described for purposes of absolution or of pleasure,
but that in both cases the speaker is responding to an injunction
to tell all. DeSade and the anonymous Victorian author are marginalized by society, but their act of turning sex into discourse
reflects a mainstream phenomenon.

Power in bourgeois society did not act mainly to repress or to
silence a sexuality which nonetheless expresses itself as all instincts
must. Rather, such power resulted in the "multiplication of singular
sexualities" (*HS* 47). Such multiplication begins with the creation
of the category of "unnatural" sexuality. Through the end of the
eighteenth century, marriage was the focus of laws, rules, and rec-
ommendations pertaining to sex. "The marriage relation was . . .
under constant surveillance: if it was found to be lacking, it had to
come forward and plead its case before a witness" (*HS* 37). Thus,
for example, the inability to fulfill the sexual duties of marriage
could be judged as a violation of the law just as adultery was so
judged. The law made only relative distinctions between sins such
as debauchery, rape, adultery, incest, and sodomy. It is true that
the category of "sins against nature" had long existed in Christian
theology, but it included crimes such as usury that had nothing to
do with sex. Sexual acts contrary to nature may have been punished
more severely, but they were still, in a fundamental sense, violations
of the law. There was such an identity between nature and the law
that physically deformed individuals, hermaphrodites, for example,
could be classified as criminals. In the nineteenth century, however,
marriage ceased to be the focus of sexual control. The legitimate
couple now became the norm against which all other sexuality was
to be compared. The sex of children, of the mad, of those who were
attracted to the same sex, now became the focus of scrutiny. Thus
various kinds of sexuality were distinguished, and those that were
unnatural were set apart. "This kind of activity assumed an auton-
omy with regard to the other condemned forms such as adultery or
rape (and the latter were condemned less and less)" (*HS* 39). Now
adultery, sodomy, sadism, and incest were all regarded as essentially
different.

Foucault's point is that we tend to identify prohibition and control, and therefore neglect the other ways in which control may be

exerted. Children's sexuality, for example, was not in the nineteenth century dealt with by simple prohibition, as adultery had been. For one thing, a child's masturbation was not regarded as a violation of law, but as a matter that needed medical treatment or parental discipline. Thus childhood onanism was treated as if it were an epidemic for which a cause must be found so that it could be eliminated. But the effect of this effort was to drive masturbation into hiding where it could then be "discovered." Where the sex of children had once been taken for granted by society, in becoming the object of intense scrutiny it became an even larger threat.

The medicalization of sex helped to create other sexual specializations. Previously, homosexual acts were condemned as sodomy, but they were treated as isolated acts. But just as the penal system had transformed the one who had committed a crime into a delinquent with a biography, so nineteenth-century medicine created the homosexual, who was also a case history and a life form. His entire being was affected by his sexuality. Thus homosexuality stopped being the mere practice of sodomy, and became "a kind of interior androgyny, a hermaphrodism of the soul. The sodomite had been a temporary aberration; the homosexual was now a species" (*HS* 43). But many other species were also "discovered." Thus aberrant sexualities were not excluded from discourse; rather, discourse gave each a local habitation and a name.

The dominant form taken by sexual discourse Foucault calls *scientia sexualis* (sexual science). He contrasts *scientia sexualis* with the *ars erotica* of societies such as China, Japan, India, and ancient Rome. In *ars erotica,* "truth is drawn from pleasure itself, understood as a practice and accumulated as experience" (*HS* 57). *Ars erotica* is thus the erotic art, and it consists not of rules, laws, or norms, but of methods. Instead of forbidding or permitting, or distinguishing and naming, it evaluates pleasure, its intensity, its duration, and its qualities. This erotic art is not attained by surveillance or inquiry, but by initiation into a body of lore that leads to a mastery of its secrets; in this the erotic arts might be considered as parallel to the martial arts. The Indian *Kama Sutra* is perhaps the best-known example of *ars erotica* in the West.

According to Foucault, the Western societies are the only ones where sexual truth takes the form of a discourse diametrically opposed to *ars erotica:* the confession. It is not surprising that Foucault should find the confession to be central to the deployment of sexuality, for the confession fuses the two forms of subjectivity that Foucault first described in his account of the human sciences in *The Order of Things*. "The confession is a ritual of discourse in which the speaking subject is also the subject of the statement; it is also a ritual that unfolds within a power relationship, for one does not confess without the presence (or virtual presence) of a partner who is not simply the interlocutor but the authority who requires the confession" (*HS* 61). In *Discipline and Punish* we saw how the disciplinary techniques could constitute the individual as an object to be judged, measured, and examined. In *The History of Sexuality*, we see how the individual is constituted as a speaking and desiring subject with an inner realm of experience that the confession reveals. But we also see that in this moment of self-expression, the individual remains the subject (that is, one who is ruled) of the priest, or, later, of the human scientist (doctor, psychiatrist, psychologist, etc.) who requires the confession. Both *ars erotica* and *scientia sexualis* involve a power relation. In the former it is the relation of the teacher who passes down his wisdom to the pupil, or of the master who initiates the novice; but in the latter, the truth comes from below, handed up to the authority who demands it.

Thus when the confession stops being exclusively the rite of penance and becomes a standard technique for authorities of all kinds, it also becomes the basis for an archive, a body of recorded knowledge. The confessions of the Christian ritual were secret; as unrecorded discourse they did not yield such an archive. But the sciences of medicine, psychiatry, and pedagogy in the nineteenth century compiled and classified the pleasures, especially the deviant pleasures, that were described to them. This was an odd sort of science since it relied not on observation and experimentation, but on the questionable evidence of introspection and lived experience. Nevertheless, a science of sexuality was produced by a fusion of the traditional procedures of the confession and the more recent techniques of the scientific disciplines. Foucault lists five ways in which the confession was transformed into science. First, the confession was combined with the examination. What the individual reported was treated as a set of signs or symptoms to be deciphered. Instead of merely asking for a recollection of deeds and desires, the scientist used manifold techniques: questionnaires, interrogation, hypnosis, free association, etc. Second, sex was posited as having vast causal powers. The most minor event in one's sexual history could have enormous consequences in any area of one's life. This justified the injunction to tell all. Third, the sexual causes for things not only were hidden, but there were forces that tended to keep them hidden. Because of this latency, the truth of sex needed to be extracted rather than merely observed. Fourth, the meaning of one's sexual report was not self-evident to the speaker, but needed to be interpreted. The one who listened to the report validated its truth by subjecting it to methods of deciphering. Fifth, the act of confession was treated as a medical procedure of diagnosis and therapy. Thus sex was no longer understood in terms merely of sin or transgression, but increasingly in those of the normal or the pathological. Who were the scientists who created and used these procedures? Foucault mentions such figures as Havelock Ellis and Kraft-Ebing who compiled descriptions of thoughts and behavior. But the procedures themselves are today most associated with another scientist, Sigmund Freud. Psychoanalysis for Foucault is not the revolutionary method Freud claimed it to be, but rather the combination of procedures developed earlier. Foucault therefore describes his history of sexuality as "an archaeology of psychoanalysis" (*HS* 130).

The discourse that is produced by the confession in both its religious and scientific forms is the sexuality that is deployed in Western societies beginning in the eighteenth century. Thus sexuality, as Foucault argued of man himself in *The Order of Things,* is a relatively recent invention. Previously, relations between the sexes were governed by the deployment of alliance, "a system of marriage, of fixation and development of kinship ties, of transmission of names and possessions" (*HS* 106). To understand what Foucault means by alliance, we might take the arranged marriages of the European aristocracy as a representative instance. These marriages were alliances of power and property. Their end was to preserve both of these for the families that the marriages allied. The whole system of alliance was intended to reproduce existing relations of power, property, and the sexes. Therefore it produced a system of rules defining the permitted and the forbidden, the licit and the illicit. It was concerned with the legal relations of partners; their physical relations were only an aspect of this larger field. Adultery was forbidden because it threatened the legal alliance, while reproductive sex between married partners was encouraged because it produced heirs that strengthened the alliance.

Sexuality differs on all of these points. Its effect is not to reproduce existing relationships, but to proliferate power by expanding the areas and forms of control. Thus it creates new relations of bodies to each other. Instead of the legal bonds between individuals, sexuality "is concerned with the sensations of the body, the quality of pleasures, and the nature of impressions" (*HS* 106). Economically speaking, sexuality treats the body as a site of production and consumption, and it seeks not to preserve wealth, but to increase and control it by controlling populations. Thus in describing sexuality as a historical construct, Foucault shows a connection between an intensification of the most private sensations and the increasing management of the behavior of large groups. The sexual individual seeks to increase his or her own pleasure through relations with the partner, while at the same time the individual is controlled by the system of knowledge based on what individuals themselves have uttered. The effect of creating a species, the homosexual, is not to repress homosexual activity—although homosexuals themselves may be persecuted—but to incite it. Paradoxically, increased control comes not from prohibition, but from proliferation.

The deployment of sexuality did not replace the deployment of alliance; sexuality was deployed on top of the already existing system of alliance. Thus the family, the institution on which alliance was founded, became the locus of sexuality. But it did so at the expense of losing its privileged status as the locus of economic, political, and social power. It became instead a cell that contained the relations of husband and wife, and parent and child, through which sexuality was deployed. Here again, psychoanalysis, with its assumption that an individual's personality takes shape as a result of the actual and imagined sexual relations of members of the family cell, provides a strong example. "The family is the interchange of sexuality and alliance: it conveys the law and the juridical dimension in the deployment of sexuality; and it conveys the economy of pleasure and the intensity of sensations in the regime of alliance" (*HS* 108). Under the increasing deployment of sexuality, then, the family has become less a locus of power and more a locus of feelings and love, a haven in a heartless world. But the family also is the point of conflict between alliance and sexuality, a conflict that Foucault finds illustrated in the modern preoccupation with the incest taboo. The locus of sexuality in the family makes sexuality always already incestuous. The system of alliance prohibits incest because in incest there is no alliance with another family. But in the sexualized family, the prohibition of incest represents merely the continued power of the system of alliance itself. By claiming that the incest taboo is foundational to all cultures, the system of alliance is preserved under the guise of natural law. Characteristically, Foucault ascribes one of the great intellectual "discoveries" of the human sciences to needs produced by those sciences themselves.

To speak of the "deployment" of sexuality is to suggest that sexuality was, like a tool or weapons system, put into service or action in someone's interest. Foucault does not mean that it could have been formulated in advance, as most tools are, but he does argue that like many other systems, its development served the interests of those in political and economic power. But, while sexuality is deployed by the bourgeoisie in their own interest, it is deployed not against the lower classes, but by the bourgeoisie to themselves. Instead of serving to control the laboring classes—as the repressive hypothesis had asserted—the deployment of sexuality was part of a general effort to assure the health and prolong the life of the ruling class. Thus the central event in the deployment of sexuality is the transformation of the confession from a religious discourse to a medical one: "instead of the question of death and everlasting punishment—the problem of life and illness. The flesh was brought down to the level of the organism" (*HS* 117). As a matter of health, sexuality was applied to those whom it was most important to keep healthy: the bourgeoisie. The laboring classes became subject to sexuality only gradually after its deployment had been completed in the ranks of their rulers.

Thus it was the bourgeois family that was first saturated with sex, and it was the bourgeois woman who, made idle by her prohibition from the economic world, was first sexualized by being charged with conjugal and parental obligations. The sexualized woman is not the same as the woman as sex object, although these two phenomena are related. Prior to the development of capitalism and the industrial system of production, women were important contributors to economic production. A large percentage of goods were produced in the home, usually for use there. But as production of products such as fabric and clothing became industrialized, more and more women found themselves idled. These women were sexualized in the sense that their sole mission in life was to produce and rear children.

In this enforced idleness, many women developed nervous disorders that were called by a variety of names but which can all be described as part of the hysterization of women's bodies. These disorders were attributed to women's sexual organs; the word *hysteria* derives from the Greek word for "uterus." Thus a pathology was believed to be intrinsic to women's bodies and women became increasingly dominated by a medicine that, in effect, nurtured and spread this pathology.[1] Since the disease was rooted in female anatomy, it could not be eliminated: all the more reason for it to be rigorously controlled. This medical intervention inscribed its discipline in the bodies it treated as a kind of internal surveillance. The mother and the nervous woman are the double that this hysterization produced.

The hysterical woman was not the only product of the nineteenth-century regime of sexuality. The masturbating child was born of a paradox: although children regularly engage in sexual activity, this activity is not capable of reproduction, and therefore must be unnatural. Thus children's sexuality becomes for the first time a pedagogical problem. The figure of the adult pervert results from the psychiatrization of deviant pleasures that were cataloged, evaluated on a scale of normality and pathology, and subjected to corrective technologies. Even the lawful sex of the conjugal couple became the subject of socialization. Fertility became a domain of incitements and restrictions, and couples were made to feel responsible to their society or race. Birth control practices were medically controlled under the claim that they, too, were pathological. Each of these figures is, like the delinquent, an object of knowledge and an object of power, but unlike the delinquent, each is at least just as likely to be bourgeois as not.

We recognize that these human products of sexuality have been produced by means of the disciplinary techniques Foucault described in *Discipline and Punish.* Foucault argues that the deployment of sexuality is part of the same shift in the character of political power, which he earlier illustrated with the transformation of juridical punishment from public torture to the prison. The sovereign was understood to have power over life and death, which was exercised by deciding to take a life or to let it live. The subject's life in this instance is a form of property. But under the regime of discipline, the "anatomo-politics of the human body," power no longer constituted itself as the will of the sovereign, but as a positive force that could "foster life or disallow it to the point of death" (*HS* 138–

39). But discipline is only one half of this new power over life; the other is a bio-politics of populations. It constitutes the body not as a machine but as an organism, the domain of biological processes, and it led to regulation designed to control public health, longevity, and propagation. Together the regimes of discipline and population control are labeled bio-power. "This bio-power was without question an indispensable element in the development of capitalism; the latter would not have been possible without the controlled insertion of bodies into the machinery of production and the adjustment of the phenomenon of population to economic processes" (*HS* 140–41).

But sexuality is implicated by Foucault in the rise of a much more overt and familiar form of domination, modern racism and its expression as a political system in fascism. He discusses this change in terms of the symbolic opposition of blood and the law. The nobility understood its caste identity in terms of blood, a history of ancestry and alliances, but "the bourgeoisie's 'blood' was its sex" (*HS* 124). Its concern for its own self-preservation focused on heredity rather than mere genealogy. This concern produced eugenics, the attempt to eliminate inferior traits through selective breeding, and a racism that would describe whole races as sources of inferior heredity. The results of the combination of eugenics and racism are to be found in Hitler's attempt to murder all of those deemed inferior. But this eugenic racism remains an expression of the symbolics of blood even as it made use of the devices of sexuality. The justification for regulating the body, health, private conduct—all aspects of everyday life—was "the mythical concern with protecting the purity of the blood and ensuring the triumph of the race" (*HS* 149).

Thus the transition from one regime to another does not occur without overlapping, without mixed forms of power. A second combination of the old sovereignty with the new sexuality leads not to eugenics and racism but to psychoanalysis. Foucault argues that in the late eighteenth century when eugenics and modern racism emerge, de Sade is describing sex as a force without any of its own norms or rules, save only an unrestricted power. Psychoanalysis begins with this same conception of sex but attempts to reinscribe it in the law. While fascism used the techniques of disciplinary power in the service of the lawless force of blood, psychoanalysis attempts to contain the unrestricted force of sex in the law of sovereignty. Psychoanalysis was thus capable of understanding fascism and its dangers. But psychoanalysis is also on the same grounds a backward-looking theory. It cannot conceptualize sexuality in terms of the formation of power contemporary with it.

The Sadian notion of sex as a lawless force, which in Freud becomes the only slightly more lawful "instinct," returns us to the issue of sex as a natural reality. Sex understood in this way could be taken as a historical constant against which cultural changes occur. But Foucault will not allow sex as an extradiscursive reality anymore than he will accept sexuality as such: "it is precisely this idea of sex *in itself* that we cannot accept without examination" (*HS* 152, italics in original). Sex, Foucault suggests, is the creation of sexuality, not the reverse. Sex conceived as a power that dominates us and as a secret that is fundamental to our being turns out to be "the most speculative, most ideal, and most internal element in a deployment of sexuality organized by power in its grip on bodies and their materiality, their forces, energies, sensations, and pleasures" (*HS* 155). Sex turns out to be yet another illusion of depth. It is thus the ironic triumph of this power for our liberation to be understood in terms of this sex. If the deployment of sexuality is to be resisted it cannot be by the act of freeing sex to take its natural course, but rather by championing the multiplicity of pleasures and the body as the site of those pleasures.

The History of Sexuality, then, does not finally assert that the desires, the acts, and the pleasures that we call sexual have been undominated. Foucault is arguing rather that the notion of repression is misleading on at least two counts. One is that it suggests that sex has become silenced or prohibited, when the true effects of sexuality have been to turn desire into discourse and to incite sexual acts. The second is that sex should not be understood as a natural force that, having been bottled up by taboos and restrictions, needs to be liberated. Rather our pleasures have been dominated by a power that seeks to manipulate them for its own ends. While Foucault is not proposing a program or movement, he does argue that this domination cannot be resisted unless sex and sexuality are understood as cultural constructions of the modern *episteme,* and that the domain they cover has been constituted in different terms in other areas and cultures.

The Later Volumes

The subsequent volumes in *The History of Sexuality* were intended to demonstrate this historical and cultural diversity. Originally, however, the series was to cover the same historical terrain with which Foucault was concerned in his other major works: the period from the Renaissance through the beginnings of the twentieth century. The volumes were to be distributed over this terrain topically, their proposed titles being: *The Flesh and the Body; The Children's Crusade; Woman, the Mother and the Hysteric; The Perverts;* and *Population and Races.*[2] As these titles indicate, the volumes in this plan would have developed in historical detail the central concepts of volume 1. But these volumes never got written. The project as a whole remained unfinished at Foucault's death. Two additional volumes were published just before he died, however, but these volumes take the project and Foucault's work in surprising new directions that, to many, are not particularly satisfying. Volume 2, *The Use of Pleasure,* discusses sexual practices in Greek antiquity, while volume 3, *The Care of the Self,* covers the Roman world of the first two centuries A.D. Thus the first major change is the vastly increased historical scope of the project. Foucault was not a specialist in ancient history, and in dealing with Greek materials he was forced to rely on translations. Perhaps because he was not a specialist, his discussions of these earlier periods have deviated far less from the standard accounts than much of his other work.[3]

During the period he was working on these later volumes, Foucault both understood himself to be entering a new area of study and revised his conception of his life's work: "I have sought to study—it is my current work—the way a human being turns him- or herself into a subject. For example, I have chosen the domain of sexuality—how men have learned to recognize themselves as subjects of 'sexuality.' Thus, it is not power, but the subject, which is the general theme of my research."[4] We have, of course, seen that the subject has been a significant preoccupation in Foucault's work since *The Order of Things.* But we should also note that Foucault said several years earlier that power was the major focus of his work. What we find in volumes 2 and 3 of *The History of Sexuality* is a broadening of the conception of the subject to the point where it can be called a self. In *The Order of Things* the subject was mainly an epistemic fiction, one of man's doubles, although Foucault correctly points out that the human sciences with which the book deals "objectivize" the subject in different ways.[5] In *Discipline and Punish,* the subject is understood as the product of a relation of dominance either to a sovereign or to the disciplinary regime. To be a subject in this sense is to be subjected. This view of the subject remains

present in volume 1 of *The History of Sexuality,* but in the later
volumes, the focus shifts to ethics. The materials that Foucault
interprets in *The Use of Pleasure,* for example, are not depicted as
imposed on the subject, but as providing him with options. In the
later volumes, then, the subject begins to have agency, the power
to make choices and set goals. But no theory of the subject or self
emerges from these volumes either. In part this is because Foucault
does continue to believe that human beings are different in different
historical eras. Thus although subjects may make themselves, they
must work with the materials their culture provides them.

There is also a change in Foucault's approach to the material. *The
Use of Pleasure* and *The Care of the Self* exhibit few of the strategies
that have characterized Foucault's writing. Although *The Use of
Pleasure* does contain a reversal of the popular conception of antiquity
as a period of dionysian sexual freedom, it is not a reversal of scholarly
studies of the period. Furthermore, the correction of this misconception
is presented as something that Foucault himself was surprised to learn. He went to Greek antiquity to find what he expected
to be a radically different construction of sexuality, but found instead
one that was indeed different but not in all of the ways he expected.
For example, both volumes detail concerns with health and well-
being which seem to undermine some of Foucault's claims in volume
1 where these concerns are depicted as emerging in the context of
the modern regime of discipline. Most importantly, Foucault discovers that Greek and Roman writing deals with sexuality in ethical
terms. Thus although sex is not a matter of sin in these cultures,
it is not treated as something that should be enjoyed indiscriminately.

Perhaps the most noticeable change in approach is the new historical strategy that emerges in the later two volumes. Instead of
focusing on ruptures, Foucault now depicts something like "epistemic drift."[6] Thus he describes a slow mutation of attitudes and
practices from paganism to Christianity. The Roman attitudes of
the era covered by *The Care of the Self* already anticipate the Christian
ones that will become dominant several hundred years later. These
changes are endearing to more traditionally minded scholars—Merquior says almost nothing positive about Foucault until he takes up
The Use of Pleasure and *The Care of the Self*—but they also mitigate
the books' impact. Where volume 1 drew wide, and mostly positive,
attention, the later volumes have been greeted in the English-speak-

ing world with generally negative reviews that suggest that the books' chief failing is their lack of intellectual excitement.

The generally negative reception of the late volumes of *The History of Sexuality* may lead us to reconsider the issue of authorship, with which this study began, by looking at the way Michel Foucault has been or is being constructed as an author. According to the rules Foucault himself borrows from Saint Jerome, the later volumes might be said to fall outside of his oeuvre, just as his early book on psychiatry is also generally excluded. But what are the major differences between these later volumes and the work that has been regarded as central? One difference is obviously the historical period with which they deal, but such a difference is probably not crucial since Foucault has usually been at odds with other authorities on Renaissance through nineteenth-century European history. The second difference I have noted is in the abandonment of many of the distinctive discursive strategies that characterized the other volumes. If this difference does in fact make *The Use of Pleasure* and *The Care of the Self* among the least read of Foucault's works over the long run, it will ironically confirm many of Foucault's own claims about the character of discursive regimes. Even Foucault's own discourse, which is contained by no single discipline or discursive formation, becomes understood as a discursive regime of its own. Thus for something to be in the Foucauldian truth it must be said using Foucauldian strategies. To put this another way, rhetoric rather than truth or ideology will be what identifies the central works of Foucault's corpus.

Chapter Eight

Conclusion: Four or Five Things to Do with Foucault

It is usual for the reader of a social critic to demand upon hearing the criticism, so what? Foucault is, as we have seen, a critic of our society and of its cultural history. But readers of Foucault are consistently frustrated by the fact that he fails to respond in any but the vaguest conceivable terms to their demand to know what action or program he would recommend to solve the problems he so effectively illustrates. To understand this failure, we need to keep in mind Foucault's skepticism. Foucault is often called a nihilist, but John Rajchman argues persuasively that Foucault "is the great skeptic of our times. . . . Foucault's philosophy does not aim for sure truths, but for the freedom of withholding judgment on philosophical dogma, and so of acquiring relief from the restrictions they introduce into our lives and our thought."[1] It is this "freedom of philosophy" that Foucault's work can give us. But in recognizing this, we also must recognize what it does not even try to give us in spite of the promises we read into it.

The first thing that Foucault does not promise is truth. Most writers and thinkers strive hard, or give the appearance of doing so, to say exactly and only what is true. They do not claim that what they write is absolute or error-free, but that their goal is to achieve something like this, at least on some small point. Foucault does not ask us to take him in this way. In a note appended to an interview he stated, "What I have said here is not 'what I think,' but often rather what I wonder whether one couldn't think" (*PK* 145). This describes the way all of his books should be read. In this same spirit he has called his work "fiction," not in the sense that it has been made up out of his imagination like a novel, but because it does not fall within the current regime of truth (*PK* 193). For Foucault, truth is a category of power; it is not an epistemological category. This does not mean that Foucault believes no distinctions between true or false can be made; on the contrary, he assumes that we must make such distinctions all the time. What he does not do is tell us how we can or should make these distinctions. Instead, he details the procedures that have been used and the effects these have had. Foucault's project asks questions about what it means to call something true. These kinds of questions cannot help us learn how to distinguish the true from the false.

The fact that Foucault eschews this problem means that he has not engaged in the task we most expect of modern philosophy, epistemology.[2] But it is hard for people not to assume that all philosophers are epistemologists, and so they take Foucault to be asserting that if truth cannot be separated from the power it always carries with it deriving from its very designation as truth, then there can be no truth. Philosophers who are epistemologists so easily catch Foucault in the self-contradictions of his historicism, relativism, etc., one would think that they would realize that Foucault could only be so easily caught in such sophomoric traps if he were not trying to avoid them.[3] All skeptical positions are self-contradictory since to be skeptical means to not offer foundations for one's own claims to truth. If one believes that foundations for truth claims are what philosophy needs to provide, then one will not find Foucault of much use.

As social criticism, Foucault's work often bears on political questions, and in some interviews he has addressed political matters directly. His frequent discussion of power also takes him into what has heretofore been considered political terrain. But Foucault's work is not a politics in any usual sense of the term. Thus Walzer misreads Foucault when he claims that the latter continues to assume traditional political categories without acknowledging them.[4] One can read Foucault politically—and it may be useful on occasion to do so—but such a reading will always put him in a bad light. Rajchman calls Foucault postrevolutionary in the sense that he rejects traditional left-wing theories that claim that a utopian society can be constructed if the state can be captured.[5] But one can go further than this and call Foucault simply postpolitical if one understands politics to be a particular historical construction that emerged from the Enlightenment. Such politics sought to provide a ground for the legitimacy of state power, and it found such ground in the consent of the governed. Political theory continues to assume that power is centered in the sovereignty of the state, an assumption Foucault has criticized by saying that "we need to cut off the King's head: in political theory that has still to be done" (*PK* 121).

In divorcing the issue of power from sovereignty and the state, Foucault rejects both bourgeois liberalism with its theory of rights divided between the state and individuals, and the Marxist theory that the state should be the representation of the interests of the people. Marxist and bourgeois politics appear as twins, each claiming that the sovereignty of the state derives from "the people," and therefore that people can change society by changing the state. To contribute to the discussion of politics is to offer opinions about who or what should be sovereign in a society; but since Foucault does not believe that power is centered in a sovereign state, he has nothing to add to this discussion. Foucault's rejection of politics carries with it serious limitations. As I noted earlier, Foucault says that he favors local and continuous action to bring about small changes, but his work does little to encourage or instruct anyone interested in undertaking such action.

If Foucault can neither offer us the solace of truth nor the comfort of revolution, what does he offer? The many commentators on his work have disagreed on the character of Foucault's central theme or major contribution, "the core meaning of his work."[6] But even to ask the question of core meaning may be to attempt to impose a closure on Foucault's work that it resists. Although Foucault's own account of the author-function would suggest the inevitability of some unity being imposed as his own disparate texts now become an oeuvre, such unity might be more legitimately discovered in the strategies common to many of them. Such unity should not be sought in a traditional theory of something, such as a theory of power, or in a methodology, such as archaeology. Foucault has explicitly denied that he is offering a theory of power because such a project would oblige one to "view [power] as emerging at a given place and time" (*PK* 199). Foucault's analysis of power is not a theory because it does not claim to be "a context-free, historical, objective description."[7] Thus Foucault's writing about power cannot be distilled down to a single account, but consists of disparate descriptions of different "powers" in different contexts. The most that can be said is that power exists in a certain way at this time in a particular domain. Similarly, the methods that one might assert as the core of Foucault's work do not really fit that role. The only methodological book, *The Archaeology of Knowledge*, does not describe a method that Foucault actually follows, or which anyone else is likely to follow. Archaeology is more effective as a metaphorical description of Foucault's approach to history than as a systematic procedure for writing history. Genealogy, Foucault's more recent name for his approach to history, is borrowed from Nietzsche. Although Foucault has modified Neitzsche's conception in several important ways, he discusses genealogy directly in few locations, most notably in the essay "Nietzsche, Genealogy, History."

Instead of providing us with theories or methods, Foucault provides us with what Gilles Deleuze called in a conversation with Foucault, "a box of tools."[8] While "tools" may imply particular descriptions of raw materials or methods for dealing with them, tools are first and foremost used to do things with. If we conceive of Foucault as providing us with tools rather than with truth or with political solutions, then we recognize that what Foucault is good for will be in part a matter of what we use him for. Foucault has, as it were, already begun to put himself to some uses that we may wish to follow, while others are projects that he barely suggests. Here then are four or five things that one could do with the tools Foucault has given us.

1. **Write or rewrite the history of a discipline.** This is one project Foucault himself had already begun to use his own tools for. And yet his usual pattern is not to deal with a discipline directly, but rather to describe its archaeology, which in this instance means the layers of intellectual sediment upon which it is built. Thus *Madness and Civilization* gives us the prehistory of psychiatry, while *The Order of Things* gives us the background of numerous human sciences. Only *The Birth of the Clinic* actually gives a detailed history of an established discipline, and even here the history covers only a relatively short part of its life. But Foucault has provided us with more than these models. First, he has given us motive to undertake this kind of research. If knowledge is always historically contingent, then we need to understand how disciplines have constituted their objects differently in different periods. In this Foucault is not alone, for the work of people such as Kuhn, Canguilhem, Feyerabend, and others also suggested this motive. Second, Foucault's archaeology suggests that a discipline's discourse, its rhetoric, limits and determines what it can and will say. Third, Foucault's new definition of "discipline" itself can help distinguish modern divisions of knowl-

edge. Not too long ago, the history of academic disciplines was regarded as a trivial task. Foucault's work has helped to demonstrate its interest and its importance.

2. **Re-evaluate the field of rhetoric.**   Rhetoric has since Plato been a poor sister to logic. Poststructuralists from Jacques Derrida to Stanley Fish have argued that this valorization of logic is based on an idealist metaphysics that is now untenable. Thus they have argued that we must understand any set of beliefs or body of knowledge as a function of the rhetorical conventions or tropes with which they must be constructed. Foucault's archaeology can add a significant new dimension to this project. While theorists such as Derrida and Paul de Man construe rhetoric to be a matter primarily of tropes— metaphor, metonymy, irony, etc.—Foucault can return rhetoric to its earlier sense as a form of persuasion and thus of power. Conversely, Foucault's characterization of bodies of knowledge as discursive formations or discursive practices identifies them with their embodiment in language instead of treating them as mere ideas. *The Archaeology of Knowledge* analyzes knowledge as a rhetorical, rather than a logical, field. It asks not why a certain body of knowledge is true or consistent, but why it is persuasive or believable, dominant or marginal. Given the fact of a general, cross-disciplinary increase in interest in rhetoric, nowhere more apparent than in the field of English, Foucault's work once again may be considered a distinctive contribution to the remaking of knowledge in this age.

3. **Reconceptualize contemporary politics.**   I said earlier that Foucault does not offer a politics, but he does suggest that the current division between socialism and democracy is no longer a useful way to conceive of our alternatives. Foucault scandalized liberals when he asserted that there is an identity between the disciplinary technologies of the West and the techniques of the Stalinist gulag. But he also scandalized Leftists when he asserted that Stalinism is not an aberration, but a product of Marxist theory (*PK* 135). Foucault suggests that power operates more similarly in democratic and socialist countries than the ideologies of either would be willing to admit. Thus Foucault's work seems to demand an historical analysis showing how the politics of socialism and the politics of democracy are a product of the same *episteme*. But he does not actually perform this analysis. Nor does he reveal what if anything he thinks might come after politics. However, his account of how contemporary power is spread throughout society in the form

of numerous practices and discourses does suggest that whatever replaces politics will locate its points of confrontation across this vast field of domination, rather than in the state or in a particular class. Foucault does not tell us how to replace politics, but he may provide the tools to help us create a plan.

4. **Add Foucault and stir.** Many readers of Foucault are not ready to adopt his skepticism, and they will continue for practical or theoretical reasons—Foucault would insist these are the same—to accept modern political or philosophical positions that Foucault himself questioned or rejected. Nevertheless, many of these readers find in Foucault's work a useful corrective to errors in the traditions of which they remain a part. For example, Mark Poster argues in *Foucault, Marxism and History* that Foucault "offers the most advanced positions available for the reconstitution of critical theory and history."[9] Poster derives from Foucault a revision of Marxist historical stages, the modes of production, which he calls modes of information. Foucault provides Poster with a perspective from which to criticize Marxism's "totalizing," its conception of history as an all-encompassing process, the class struggle, in terms of which all events and ideas are judged. But Poster remains committed to revolutionary class struggle, and he therefore does not accept Foucault's claim that revolution is an illusory goal: "Foucault's discourse analysis, whatever its merits, cannot replace class analysis."[10] Because Foucault has not created a system or a method, his work lends itself to the modification of existing intellectual practices. Or perhaps . . .

5. **Resist disciplinary power.** Foucault's analysis of micropower is like a manual for the resister who remains inside the disciplinary institutions. I am not speaking only of prisoners or mental patients here, but of employees, students, teachers, all those whose bodies and souls are subject to repeated examination and normalizing judgment. Consider the modern professions, for example. Doctors, lawyers, engineers, and teachers all command our attention and respect—and thus have power over us—because they claim some kind of exclusive expertise. We listen to a doctor, and pay him handsomely for his advice, because we are confident that he knows more than you or I or an engineer about our bodies and diseases. We listen to the generals and bureaucrats from the Department of Defense and are likely to accept, also on the grounds of specialized expertise, that we do need another weapons system.

But in each case a form of disciplinary power is being exercised over us that we cannot resist unless we recognize that it is power and not truth that is spoken in each case. This does not mean that we will always choose to resist, and in fact it is Foucault's point that such total resistance is impossible. But it is also Foucault's point that resistance is integral to discipline and hence inevitable. Thus, resistance to disciplinary power is paradoxically both the least and the most Foucauldian thing to do with Foucault. If such resistance is inevitable, then it is likely to be of little consequence, and it is unnecessary to be reminded of its possibility here. On the other hand, such resistance seems that to which Foucault himself describes his own position as leading, "a hyper- and pessimistic activism."[11]

The conception of Foucault's work as a tool kit is somewhat misleading. While his work does not offer a take-it-or-leave-it system, to conceive of thoughts as tools is already to have accepted some of Foucault's skeptical premises. If one is convinced that objectivity is possible in the social sciences or philosophy, and thus that theories of power are possible, then one will not be satisfied by mere tools or strategies. Rhetoric will not be of interest, except as a matter of mere form, and the history of science will still seem to be the useless recollection of discarded theories. But philosophers, scientists, and other intellectuals had begun to question this positivist epistemology long before Foucault came on the scene. There will be many, then, who will find things to do with his tools.

Notes and References

Chapter One

1. Roland Barthes, "The Death of the Author," in *Image, Music, Text,* trans. Stephen Heath (New York: Hill and Wang, 1977), 145.

2. "What is an Author?," in *Language, Counter-Memory, Practice,* ed. Donald F. Bouchard (Ithaca, N.Y.: Cornell University Press, 1977), 121. Subsequent references to "What is an Author?" (identified as *W*) will be made parenthetically in the text.

3. *The Birth of the Clinic,* trans. A. M. Sheridan Smith (New York: Pantheon, 1973), xvi. Subsequent references to this book (identified as *BC*) will be made parenthetically in the text.

4. *The Archaeology of Knowledge,* trans. A. M. Sheridan Smith (New York: Pantheon, 1972), 17. Subsequent references to this book (identified as *AK*) will be made parenthetically in the text.

5. Quoted by Otto Friedrich, with Sandra Burton, in "France's Philosopher of Power," *Time* 16 November 1981, 148.

6. Alan Sheridan, *Michel Foucault: The Will to Truth* (London: Travistock, 1980), 2, 4.

7. Michael Clark, *Michel Foucault, An Annotated Bibliography: Tool Kit for a New Age* (New York: Garland, 1983), xx.

8. *Power/Knowledge: Selected Interviews and Other Writings 1972–1977,* ed. Colin Gordon, trans. Colin Gordon, et al. (New York: Pantheon, 1980), 66. Subsequent references to this book (identified as *PK*) will be made parenthetically in the text.

9. *The Order of Things: An Archaeology of the Human Sciences,* trans. Alan Sheridan (New York: Pantheon, 1970), 385. Subsequent references to this book (identified as *OT*) will be made parenthetically in the text.

10. Sheridan, *The Will to Truth,* 89.

11. "Nietzsche, Genealogy, History," in *Language, Counter-Memory, Practice,* 150. Subsequent references to "Nietzsche, Genealogy, History" (identified as *NGH*) will be made parenthetically in the text.

12. "The Subject and Power," afterword [1982] to Hubert Dreyfus and Paul Rabinow, *Michel Foucault: Beyond Structuralism and Hermeneutics,* 2nd ed. (Chicago: University of Chicago Press, 1983), 209.

Chapter Two

1. Sheridan, *The Will to Truth,* 215; John Rajchman, *Michel Foucault: The Freedom of Philosophy* (New York: Columbia University Press, 1985), 2.

2. "The Discourse on Language," trans. Rupert Swyer, appendix to *The Archaeology of Knowledge*, 229. Subsequent references to "The Discourse on Language" (identified as *DC*) will be made parenthetically in the text.

3. Hayden White, "Foucault's Discourse: The Historiography of Anti-Humanism," in *The Content of the Form* (Baltimore: Johns Hopkins University Press, 1987), 110.

4. *Madness and Civilization*, trans. Richard Howard (New York: Pantheon, 1965), 247. Subsequent references to this book (identified as *MC*) will be made parenthetically in the text.

5. *The History of Sexuality, Volume I: An Introduction*, trans. Robert Hurley (New York: Pantheon, 1978), 15–49. Subsequent references to volume 1 (identified as *HS*) will be made parenthetically in the text.

6. Stephen J. Gould, *Time's Arrow, Time's Cycle: Myth and Metaphor in the Discovery of Geological Time* (Cambridge, Mass.: Harvard University Press, 1987).

Chapter Three

1. Mark Cousins and Athar Hussain, *Michel Foucault* (New York: St. Martin's Press, 1984), 137–138.

2. Dreyfus and Rabinow, *Beyond Structuralism and Hermeneutics*, 12.

3. Jacques Derrida, "Cogito and the History of Madness," in *Writing and Difference*, trans. Alan Bass (Chicago: University of Chicago Press, 1978), 31–63.

4. Gerald Weismann, "Foucault and the Bag Lady," in *The Woods Hole Cantata: Essays on Science and Society* (New York: Dodd, Mead, 1985), 30–31.

5. Cousins and Hussain, *Michel Foucault*, 129.

6. Clark, *Bibliography*, 88–89.

7. Sheridan, *The Will to Truth*, 206.

8. Rajchman, *The Freedom of Philosophy*, 5.

9. Sheridan, *The Will to Truth*, 206.

10. Roland Barthes, "Taking Sides," in *Critical Essays*, trans. Richard Howard (Evanston, Ill.: Northwestern University Press, 1972), 164.

11. Sheridan, *The Will to Truth*, 37; Karlis Racevskis, *Michel Foucault and the Subversion of Intellect* (Ithaca, N.Y.: Cornell University Press, 1983), 55.

12. Dreyfus and Rabinow, *Beyond Structuralism and Hermeneutics*, 15.

13. Claude Lévi-Strauss, "The Culinary Triangle," *New Society*, 22 December 1966, 937–40. Figure adapted from Edmund Leach, *Claude Lévi-Strauss*, rev. ed. (New York: Viking, 1974), 27.

14. Martin Jay, "In the Empire of the Gaze: Foucault and the Denigration of Vision in Twentieth-Century Thought," in *Foucault: A Critical Reader*, ed. David C. Hoy (Oxford: Basil Blackwell, 1986), 181.

15. Jean-Paul Sartre, *Being and Nothingness*, trans. Hazel Barnes (New York: Philosophical Library, 1956), 252–302.

16. Martin Jay, "In the Empire of the Gaze," in *Foucault: A Critical Reader*, 176. But see Gilles Deleuze, *Foucault* (Paris: Minuit, 1986), 115–130, who argues that Foucault's treatment of the gaze is an innovation in that it separates the visible from the consciousness of the one looking.

Chapter Four

1. John Rajchman, *The Freedom of Philosophy*, 14.

2. Ibid., 25.

3. The controversy over *Las Meninas* cannot be treated in detail here. Joel Snyder, "*Las Meninas* and the Mirror of the Prince," *Critical Inquiry* 11 (1985):539–72, argues that Foucault's interpretation is wrong on the grounds that since the perspective of *Las Meninas* is "orthodox" "one-point" perspective, we can determine that "*Las Meninas* is projected from a point directly to the right of the mirror" and hence that "if we were gazing from the center of projection of *Las Meninas* at a construction of the room represented in the painting, we could not see ourselves in the mirror" (548). More recently, however, what seems certain to be the definitive study of Velázquez has appeared: Jonathan Brown, *Velázquez: Painter and Courtier* (New Haven: Yale University Press, 1987). Brown argues, on the basis of seeing the painting after a recent cleaning, that Velázquez changed the dimensions of the room after he had begun the painting and hence that the perspective is not regular, and may have been deliberately left ambiguous (259).

4. Dreyfus and Rabinow, *Beyond Structuralism and Hermeneutics*, 25.

5. Rajchman, *The Freedom of Philosophy*, 15.

6. Pamela Major-Poetzl, *Michel Foucault's Archaeology of Western Culture* (Chapel Hill: University of North Carolina Press, 1983), 149.

7. Edmund Husserl, "The Origin of Geometry," in *The Crisis of European Sciences and Transcendental Phenomenology*, trans. David Carr (Evanston, Ill.: Northwestern University Press, 1970), 353–78.

8. Theodor Adorno and Max Horkheimer, *The Dialectic of Enlightenment* (New York: Seabury, 1972); Jürgen Habermas, *Knowledge and Human Interests*, trans. Jeremy Shapiro (Boston: Beacon, 1971).

9. A. J. Greimas and F. Rastier, "The Interaction of Semiotic Constraints," *Yale French Studies* 41 (1968): 86–105. Figure adapted from Fredric Jameson, *The Prison-House of Language* (Princeton: Princeton University Press, 1972), 163.

10. Cousins and Hussain, *Michel Foucault*, 48–49.

11. Dreyfus and Rabinow, *Beyond Structuralism and Hermeneutics*, 38.

12. Ibid., 31.

13. Ibid., 17.

14. T. S. Kuhn, *The Structure of Scientific Revolutions,* 2nd ed. (Chicago: University of Chicago Press, 1970), 52–53.

15. Ernst Mayr, *The Growth of Biological Thought,* (Cambridge, Mass.: Harvard University Press, 1982), 113.

16. Ibid., 363.

17. John C. Greene, review of *Les Mots et les choses, Studies in Semiotics* 13 (1967):131–38.

18. For an overview of many of these charges see J. G. Merquior, *Foucault* (London: Collins, 1985), especially 56–75.

Chapter Five

1. *Death and the Labyrinth: The World of Raymond Roussel,* trans. Charles Raus (Garden City, N.Y.: Doubleday, 1986. Subsequent references to this book (identified as *DL*) will be made parenthetically in the text.

2. Raymond Roussel, *How I Wrote Certain of My Books,* quoted in Foucault, *Death and the Labyrinth,* 30–31.

3. Sheridan, *The Will to Truth,* 89.

4. Cousins and Hussain, *Michel Foucault,* 97.

5. Alan Megill, *Prophets of Extremity: Nietzsche, Heidegger, Foucault, Derrida* (Berkeley: University of California Press, 1985), 227–32.

6. Dreyfus and Rabinow, *Beyond Structuralism and Hermeneutics,* 49.

7. Ibid., 51.

8. Dreyfus and Rabinow, *Beyond Structuralism and Hermeneutics,* 104.

9. The passage quotes Nietzsche's *The Gay Science* and *Human, All Too Human.*

10. Stephen J. Gould, "Life's Little Joke," *Natural History* 96 (April 1987):20–21.

11. Friedrich Neitzsche, *On the Genealogy of Morals and Ecce Homo,* trans. Walter Kaufmann (New York: Random House, 1967), 34.

12. Ibid., 25–28.

13. Dreyfus and Rabinow, *Beyond Structuralism and Hermeneutics,* 97.

14. Charles C. Lemert and Garth Gillan, *Michel Foucault: Social Theory and Transgression* (New York: Columbia University Press, 1982), 138.

Chapter Six

1. Merquior, *Foucault,* 35.

2. Mark Poster, *Foucault, Marxism and History,* (Cambridge: Polity 1984), 95.

3. *Discipline and Punish: The Birth of the Prison,* trans. Alan Sheridan (New York: Pantheon, 1977), 3. Foucault quotes from the original documents of Damiens's case. Subsequent references to *Discipline and Punish* (identified as *DP*) will be made parenthetically in the text.

4. Michael Walzer, "The Politics of Michel Foucault," in *Foucault, A Critical Reader*, 64.

5. Dreyfus and Rabinow, *Beyond Structuralism and Hermeneutics*, 160.

6. This charge is made by those on all sides of the political spectrum, from Marxist critic Fredric Jameson, in *The Political Unconscious: Narrative as a Socially Symbolic Act* (Ithaca, N.Y.: Cornell University Press, 1981), 90, to a liberal such as Walzer, "The Politics of Michel Foucault," in *Foucault: A Critical Reader*, 64.

7. "The Subject and Power," afterword [1982] to *Beyond Structuralism and Hermeneutics*, 217, 221.

8. Merquior, *Foucault*, 109.

Chapter Seven

1. Barbara Ehrenreich and Deirdre English, *For Her Own Good: 150 Years of Experts' Advice to Women* (Garden City, N.Y.: Doubleday, 1978), 101–140.

2. Clark, *Bibliography*, 25.

3. Merquior, *Foucault*, 137.

4. "The Subject and Power," afterword [1982] to *Beyond Structuralism and Hermeneutics*, 208–9.

5. Ibid., 208.

6. Frances Bartkowski, "Epistemic Drift in Foucault," in *Feminism and Foucault: Reflections on Resistance*, ed. Irene Diamond and Lee Quinby (Boston: Northeastern University Press, 1988, 43–58.

Chapter Eight

1. Rajchman, *The Freedom of Philosophy*, 2.

2. Richard Rorty, "Foucault and Epistemology," in *Foucault: A Critical Reader*, 41–49.

3. Walzer, "The Politics of Michel Foucault," in *Foucault: A Critical Reader*, 64–65; Hilary Putnum, *Reason, Truth and History* (Cambridge: Cambridge University Press, 1981), 155–62.

4. Walzer, "The Politics of Michel Foulcault," in *Foucault: a Critical Reader*, 51.

5. Rajchman, *The Freedom of Philosophy*, 61–67.

6. Merquior, *Foucault*, 141–42.

7. Dreyfus and Rabinow, *Beyond Structuralism and Hermeneutics*, 184.

8. Michel Foucault and Gilles Deleuze, "Intellectuals and Power," in *Language, Counter-Memory, Practice*, 208. Foucault also uses the term in *Power/Knowledge*, 145.

9. Poster describes his own book in his essay "Foucault and the Tyranny of Greece," in *Foucault: A Critical Reader*, 205.

10. Poster, *Foucault, Marxism and History*, 90.

11. "On the Genealogy of Ethics: An Overview of Work in Progress,"
afterword (1983) to Dreyfus and Rabinow, *Beyond Structuralism and Hermeneutics,* 232.

Selected Bibliography

PRIMARY SOURCES

Books

Maladie mentale et personnalité. Paris: Presses Universitaires de France, 1954. English translation, *Mental Illness and Psychology*. Translated by Alan Sheridan. New York: Harper & Row, 1976.

Histoire de la folie à l'âge classique. Paris: Gallimard, 1972. First edition, *Folie et déraison*, published in 1961. English translation (abridged), *Madness and Civilization: A History of Insanity in the Age of Reason*. Translated by Richard Howard. New York: Pantheon, 1965.

Naissance de la clinique: une archéologie du regard médical. Paris: Presses Universitaires de France, 1963. English translation, *The Birth of the Clinic: An Archaeology of Medical Perception*. Translated by A. M. Sheridan Smith. New York: Pantheon, 1973.

Raymond Roussel. Paris: Gallimard, 1963. English translation, *Death and the Labyrinth: The World of Raymond Roussel*. Translated by Charles Raus. Garden City: Doubleday, 1986.

Les Mots et les choses: une archéologie des sciences humaines. Paris: Gallimard, 1966. English translation, *The Order of Things: An Archaeology of the Human Sciences*. Translated by Alan Sheridan. New York: Pantheon, 1970.

L'archéologie du savoir. Paris: Gallimard, 1969. English translation, *The Archaeology of Knowledge*. Translated by A. M. Sheridan Smith. New York: Pantheon, 1972.

L'ordre du discours: leçon inaugurale du Collège de France prononcé le 2 décembre 1970. Paris: Gallimard, 1971. English translation, "The Discourse on Language." Translated by Rupert Swyer. Appendix to *The Archaeology of Knowledge*.

Ceci n'est pas une pipe: deux lettres et quatre dessins de René Magritte. Montpellier, France: Fata Morgana, 1973. English translation, *This is Not a Pipe*. Translated and edited by James Harkness. Berkeley: University of California Press, 1981.

Moi, Peirre Rivière, ayant égorgé ma mère, ma soeur et mon frère . . . : un cas de parricide au XIXe siècle. Paris: Gallimard, 1973. English translation, *I, Pierre Rivière, having slaughtered my mother, my sister, and my brother . . . : A Case of Parricide in the 19th Century*. Translated by Frank Jellinek. Lincoln: University of Nebraska Press, 1975.

Surveiller et punir: naissance de la prison. Paris: Gallimard, 1975. English translation, *Discipline and Punish: The Birth of the Prison.* Translated by Alan Sheridan. New York: Pantheon, 1977.

Histoire de la sexualité, I: la volonté de savoir. Paris: Gallimard, 1976. English translation, *The History of Sexuality, Volume I: An Introduction.* Translated by Robert Hurley. New York: Pantheon, 1978.

Language, Counter-Memory, Practice: Selected Essays and Interviews. Edited by Donald F. Bouchard. Translated by Donald F. Bouchard and Sherry Simon. Ithaca, N.Y.: Cornell University Press, 1977.

Editor. *Herculine Barbin, dite Alexina B.* Paris: Gallimard, 1978. English translation, *Herculine Barbin: Being the Recently Discovered Memoirs of a Nineteenth-Century French Hermaphrodite.* With an introduction to the English edition by Foucault. Translated by Richard McDougall. New York: Pantheon, 1980.

Power/Knowledge: Selected Interviews and Other Writings 1972–1977. Edited by Colin Gordon. Translated by Colin Gordon, et al. New York: Pantheon, 1980.

Histoire de la sexualité, II: l'usage des plaisirs. Paris: Gallimard, 1984. English translation, *The Use of Pleasure,* vol. 2 of *The History of Sexuality.* Translated by Robert Hurley. New York: Pantheon, 1985.

Histoire de la sexualité, III: le Souci de soi. Paris: Gallimard, 1984. English translation, *The Care of the Self,* vol. 3 of *The History of Sexuality.* Translated by Robert Hurley. New York: Pantheon, 1986.

The Foucault Reader. Edited by Paul Rabinow. New York: Pantheon, 1984.

Uncollected Essays and Interviews

"The Subject and Power." Afterword [1982] to Hubert Dreyfus and Paul Rabinow, *Michel Foucault: Beyond Structuralism and Hermeneutics,* 2nd ed., 208–226. Chicago: University of Chicago Press, 1983.

"On the Genealogy of Ethics: An Overview of Work in Progress." An interview conducted by Hubert Dreyfus and Paul Rabinow. Afterword (1983) to *Michel Foucault: Beyond Structuralism and Hermeneutics,* 2nd ed., 229–52. Chicago: University of Chicago Press, 1983.

"Le Retour de la morale." *Les Nouvelles,* 28 June–5 July 1984, 27–41. English translation, "Final Interview." Translated by Thomas Levin and Isabelle Lorenz. *Raritan* 5 (Summer 1985):1–13.

SECONDARY SOURCES

Baudrillard, Jean. *Forget Foucault.* New York: Semiotext(e), 1987. An argument by a leading member of the current French avant-garde that Foucault's work is complicitous in the strategies that it examines.

Clark, Michael. *Michel Foucault, An Annotated Bibliography: Tool Kit for a New Age.* New York: Garland, 1983. A comprehensive bibliography of work by and about Foucault through 1982.

Certeau, Michael de. "Micro-techniques and Panoptic Discourse: A Quid pro Quo. "In *Heterologies: Discourse of the Other.* Translated by Brian Massumi. Minneapolis: University of Minnesota Press, 1986, 185– 192. A critique of Foucault's method in *Discipline and Punish.*

Cousins, Mark, and Athar Hussain. *Michel Foucault.* New York: St. Martins Press, 1984. A lucid introduction to Foucault's work.

Deleuze, Gilles. *Foucault.* Paris: Minuit, 1986. A reading of Foucault in the context continental philosophy by a leading French intellectual and ally of the author.

Dreyfus, Hubert, and Paul Rabinow. *Michel Foucault: Beyond Structuralism and Hermeneutics.* 2nd ed. Chicago: University of Chicago Press, 1983. The most successful attempt to define the place of Foucault's work in the context of contemporary philosophy and theory.

Fraser, Nancy. "Michel Foucault: A 'Young Conservative'?" *Ethics* 96 (1985):165–84. Surveys the debate initiated by Habermas's charge that Foucault was a "young conservative."

Gane, Mike, ed. *Towards a Critique of Foucault.* London: Routledge & Kegan Paul, 1986. Analysis of political issues in Foucault's work by British Leftists.

Habermas, Jürgen. "Modernity versus Postmodernity." *New German Critique* 22 (1981):3–14. Calls Foucault conservative because of his rejection of Enlightenment rationality.

Hoy, David C., ed. *Foucault: A Critical Reader.* Oxford: Basil Blackwell, 1986. Includes essays by such major figures as Richard Rorty and Jürgen Habermas. Especially good on issues of politics and power.

Lemert, Charles C., and Garth Gillan. *Michel Foucault: Social Theory and Transgression.* New York: Columbia University Press, 1982. An introduction to Foucault organized in terms of his major themes rather than his books.

Major-Poetzl, Pamela. *Michel Foucault's Archaeology of Western Culture: Toward a New Science of History.* Chapel Hill: University of North Carolina Press, 1983. Regards archaeology as a revolutionary theoretical achievement and treats it in the context of modern theories of physics.

Megill, Alan. *Prophets of Extremity: Nietzsche, Heidegger, Foucault, Derrida.* Berkeley: University of California Press, 1985. A critical look at Foucault's relation to Nietzsche, and to phenomenology and structuralism.

Merquior, J. G. *Foucault.* London: Collins, 1985. The most unsympathetic of Foucault's commentators.

Morris, Meagan, and Paul Patton, editors. *Michel Foucault: Power, Truth,*

Strategy. Sydney, Australia: Feral, 1979. Includes an excellent account of Foucault's intellectual milieu and several occasional pieces by Foucault himself.

Poster, Mark. *Foucault, Marxism and History: Mode of Production versus Mode of Information.* Cambridge: Polity, 1984. Reads Foucault's work as a critique of and contribution to Marxist theory.

Rajchman, John. *Michel Foucault: The Freedom of Philosophy.* New York: Columbia University Press, 1985. Four careful philosophical meditations on Foucault as a skeptical philosopher. Excellent.

Racevskis, Karlis. *Michel Foucault and the Subversion of Intellect.* Ithaca: Cornell University Press, 1983. A reading of Foucault informed by Lacanian and other poststructuralist theory. Contains a good account of "Critical Reactions and Challenges" to Foucault's work.

Said, Edward. "Criticism Between Culture and System." In *The World, the Text, and the Critic,* 178–225. Cambridge, Mass.: Harvard University Press, 1983. A consideration of Foucault in relation to Derrida, and of them both in relation to literary criticism by a scholar whose work has been significantly influenced by Foucault.

Sheridan, Alan. *Michel Foucault: The Will to Truth.* London: Travistock, 1980. Contains the best account of the relation of Foucault's life and work.

Smart, Barry. *Foucault, Marxism and Critique.* London: Routledge & Kegan Paul, 1983. Places Foucault in the context of contemporary Marxist theory.

————. *Michel Foucault.* Key Sociologists. Sussex, England: Ellis Horwood; London: Travistock, 1985. Considers Foucault's work as a contribution to social analysis and research.

White, Hayden. "Foucault's Discourse: The Historiography of Anti-Humanism." In *The Content of the Form,* 104–41. Baltimore: Johns Hopkins University Press, 1987. An analysis of Foucault's tropes by the leading theorist of the discourse of historians.

Wuthnow, Robert, et al. *Cultural Analysis: The Work of Peter L. Berger, Mary Douglas, Michel Foucault, and Jürgen Habermas.* London: Routledge & Kegan Paul, 1984. Treats Foucault as a neostructuralist.

Index

173